Praise for '

"My friend Dwayne Morris has written a book that every believer should read. Living for the glory of God and seeking to make his name great is truly what each of us are created for."
-Steve Wright, author of reThink and ApParent Privilege

"In a world of maintaining the 'status quo,' *the OUTRAGEOUS life* challenges us to go to the next level in our walk with God. Following these principles will produce extraordinary results in your daily life. It starts with where you are and takes you where you want to be."
-Dr. Mike Hamlet, Sr. Pastor, First Baptist North Spartanburg

"Radical life changing truths are rarely truths never before revealed. Solomon already told us there is nothing new under the sun. Sometimes truths we have already known have a radical impact on us because of the way that they are communicated. Dwayne accomplishes just that. He takes some simple ideas of knowing God and walking with God and His plan for our lives and presents them in a fresh and challenging fashion that will have you grappling anew with where you are in following the Lord."
-Dr. Randy Hahn, Sr. Pastor, Colonial Heights Baptist Church

"Dwayne's obedience and commitment to Jesus Christ has produced a wonderful book for which I am extremely grateful. His dedication to helping people get to know Jesus in a personal way spans over 20+ years of ministry. Dwayne, like Gideon, is an ordinary man that they Lord has used in extraordinary ways to draw people closer to Himself. May this book inspire you, as it has me, to continue to place all of your trust in the Lord Jesus Christ and know that if you think your plans are outrageous, wait until you see what the Lord has in store."
-Caz McCaslin, Founder and President, Upward

"Dwayne's book, I believe, will have a positive impact on everyone who reads it. He has done an incredible job expressing God's love and how we can walk in faith hearing clearly the promises and provisions taught in God's Holy Word, the Bible."
-Wallace Nix, Executive Director of Chosen Children Ministries

"God has a plan for your life. It's an incredible plan. It may sound crazy and it may sound hard, but it will blow any plan you could conceive away. All that is needed for the plan to be set in motion is for you to simply say YES! If you do, God will do extraordinary things in and through you, and He will do it in such a way that the credit could only go to Himself. Dwayne Morris nails this idea in his book *the OUTRAGEOUS life*. It is a must-read for anyone who is ready to get off the bench and into the game."
-Jon Estes, Director & CEO, Woodlands Camp

the OUTRAGEOUS life

Letting God Take You from

Ordinary to Outrageous

Dwayne Morris

ISBN:1482549840
ISBN-13:9781482549843

the OUTRAGEOUS life / by Dwayne Morris
www.MorrisMatters.com

Cover design by Barry Burnett

Author photo by Chad Lane, www.chadlanephoto.com

DEDICATION

This book is dedicated to my Heavenly Father...
...this was His idea.

Thanks to my bride and greatest friend, Angela. You saw this coming long before I did.

TABLE OF CONTENTS

INTRODUCTION

"God just asked me a question!"

These were the words Alex Kendrick spoke to his wife. Alex is the creator, director, producer, and promoter for the Sherwood films: *Facing the Giants*, *Fireproof* and *Courageous*. He is someone who has witnessed and experienced the hand of God working in ways he never expected.

"Well, what did you say?" she responded with anticipation.

"I don't know," Alex replied. "I didn't give him an answer."

The question Alex heard clearly was this:

"Alex, would you rather have an easier road with less fruit or a harder road with more fruit?"

Now, that's a challenging question. What do you think? How would you answer that question? The easy road doesn't ask for much. In a spiritual sense, there's little commitment and a lot of free time. People on this road tend to be floaters. They do as little for the

Kingdom of God as possible but enough to earn themselves a star on the chart in the Sunday School room.

The Star Chart

I remember going to church as a child and seeing this big poster on the wall that looked like the early concept drawing of an Excel chart. The left side of the chart boasted the names of everyone in the class. The top identified the columns and desired outcomes the teacher wanted us to complete every time we came to Sunday School. These included: Brought My Bible, Brought an Offering, and the most important, Attended Sunday School. Each week, we had the opportunity to put our own stars on the chart for the actions we had completed that day.

The easy road is doing as little as possible just to get your star. I'm not sure about you, but that sure seems like a shallow and uneventful spiritual life. In fact, spiritually speaking, it's outright dangerous. The person on the easy road tends to evaluate their status as a Christian based on all they do. It's very much like the group of people we find mentioned in the book of Matthew, near the end of one of the greatest sermons uttered from the lips of Jesus, the Sermon on the Mount.

The End Of The Beginning

As Jesus brings His sermon to an end, He drops this simple phrase: "Not everyone who says to me, 'Lord, Lord,' will enter the Kingdom of heaven, but he who does the will of My Father who is in heaven will enter."[1] Listen to how Eugene Peterson expresses this same passage in The Message: "Knowing the correct password—saying 'Master, Master,' for instance— isn't going to get you anywhere with me. What is required is serious obedience—doing what my Father wills."[2]

What happens next grabbed my attention many years ago as I heard this taught for the first time. Just as Jesus did throughout His entire ministry, He offered an illustration to help His audience connect with His point. He said, "Many will say to me on that day, 'Lord, Lord, did we not prophesy in your name and in your name drive out demons and in your name perform many miracles?'"[3] These people immediately defaulted to a list of all they had done. If we fast-forward this response to the present, it might sound like this: "Wait a minute, Jesus, didn't you see me in Sunday School almost every Sunday? And what about that time I gave money to the guy on the street corner? Didn't you notice when I gave some old clothes to the local mission house for homeless people? Remember that time when my friend thought she had cancer, and I prayed a lot, and it turned out the tumor was benign?"

Many people equate what they do with what they hope they are. They want to identify with Christianity and have an idea of what they need to do to wear that label. The only problem is that Jesus is not concerned about what we do as much as He is about who we know. (Yes, it really is about who you know...)

As Jesus continues His illustration, He brings everything to a sudden and revealing halt. He delivers a startling truth in verse 23: "Then I will tell them plainly, 'I never knew you. Away from me, you evildoers!'"[4] Again, Eugene Peterson's perspective is so pure: "And do you know what I am going to say? 'You missed the boat. All you did was use me to make yourselves important. You

3

don't impress me one bit. You're out of here.'"[5]

The reality of who we are as followers of Jesus Christ is not tied to what we do. It is based on if we know Him in a personal way. This is where the star on the wall sets us up for failure. We become so focused on getting a sticker star that we miss the One who created all of the real stars.

In his book *Chasing Elephants: Wrestling with the Gray Areas of Life,* Brent Crowe cites a phrase from a sermon by Bill Hybels that summarizes this notion so well. "The weak Christian is wed to a rule-oriented, mechanical-type faith." Brent goes on to add, "Simply put, at some level, people who are weak in their faith are trying to earn a relationship with God. When we base our relationship with God on morality or rules rather than transformation, we will constantly judge ourselves on what we can accomplish rather than what Christ has already accomplished in us."[6]

More Good Than Bad

The bottom line is simple: It's not about where you sit on Sunday but how you live on Monday. I must confess, that's not original. I captured it on the corner of a sheet of paper and forgot to note the source. Regardless of who said it, you have to admit that it works. We must be focused more on knowing and loving Jesus Christ Monday through Saturday than we are on just being in church on Sunday, not to mention all of the other things we attempt in order to gain enough credits to get into Heaven or to keep God from zapping us with bad luck.

As I have shared my faith with others, I've heard many say the same thing: "I hope my good just outweighs my bad." What they are saying is, "I hope I have enough credits to get into Heaven." Hope? You "hope" you get into Heaven? In this case hope is never a good strategy. As we've already seen, it takes more than having a plan. It takes a relationship built on faith - faith in God and faith that He can do something great with your life.

A Problem to Be Solved

You are about to meet a man named Gideon. His story is one of doubt, confidence, faith, obstacles, fear, plans, and battles. Wow, that sounds familiar. Can you identify with any of those? Gideon was just an ordinary guy whom God used in an outrageous way. It didn't happen overnight, and, as you may imagine, there was some resistance at first. He didn't have any special in-road with God. Nor did his parents negotiate a deal that God would give him an extra dose of potential. Gideon's story is simply about a problem that needed to be solved and how God used an ordinary person to accomplish something beyond his imagination – something outrageous.

Imagine what that looks like for you. Imagine God using you to accomplish something outrageous. Surely you have the notion that your life is meant for more than what you are getting at the moment. John 10:10 tells us that we are to have a full life. Is that how you see your life? Is it full, or is there clearly room for more?

When you think about your life, is there something that you just can't shake? Is there a nagging notion that just won't go away? It sort of sits in the bottom of your heart as a deep-seated dream. The Bible teaches us that when we place our attention and focus on the things God has for us, He will "give you the desires of our heart."[7] Could it be that He placed the desire in your heart to do that "something?" I think so.

I say that because I see it all through Scripture. God has a way of using unsuspecting individuals to do some outrageous things. Gideon was one of those people. He was God's chosen leader to do something amazing so that others could experience the power of God as never before. Gideon's experience will show us some key principles that will help us realize a life that is more than showing up on Sunday and getting a star. I prayerfully desire that by the end of our journey you will be able to come to the same realization that Alex did about his life:

"I came to realize that God can use my desire to tell stories and do more than [I] ever thought possible...only if [I] would trust him with it." – Alex Kendrick[8]

CHAPTER 1: BACKSTORY

Before We Get Too Far

If you're like me, you tend to grab a book, jump to the first chapter and launch into your reading adventure. Most often, that includes skipping the Introduction. If this is you, I suggest that you rewind a few pages and start there. It will set the foundation for the rest of our journey.

Let's Start in the Beginning

The backdrop for Gideon's story originates from an era that is preceded by the Israelite conquest of their new territory. There's a lot that led up to that moment. In fact, let's just go back to the beginning...to the Garden of Eden.

"In the beginning God created the Heavens and the Earth."[1] Soon after this event, He created Adam and Eve and gave them their purpose statement: "Be fruitful, multiply and replenish the earth...."[2] As you know, God was not telling them to be sure to work on the times

7

tables, but they were responsible for populating the planet. Now, that's a pretty tall order.

The First Family

Fast-forward to a man by the name of Abraham. He was to become known as the Father of the Jewish nation. God made it clear that he would have a lot of children. I guess you could say he was the predecessor to The Learning Channel's Duggar family, but he was promised a few more children than the Duggars. In fact, God told Abraham if he wanted to know how many children he would have, he should go count the stars.[3]

Abraham became known as the Father of the Jews. As you work through his family tree, you meet the rest of the key descendants that many are familiar with from the Bible: Isaac, Jacob, and Joseph. There's also a geographical trail that can be followed. As the descendants of Abraham increased in number, they were constantly moving to find more space.

Moving Day

The most significant move came when Joseph was in a position of authority in Egypt, second only to the king. He relocated his entire family from their home in Canaan to Egypt. Once settled, they continued to grow as a family and a nation. This line of the family of Abraham and the Jewish nation remained in Egypt for 400 years.

As you might imagine, a family with the blessing and covenant from God to have as many descendants as the stars and grains of sand; plus, 400 years time can create a lot of people. In fact, it created a problem for the new leadership in Egypt. The king became concerned that the Jews could soon reach a population so large that, were

Egypt to be attacked by another nation, the Jews would join the invading military and overtake Egypt.

Hope Floats

The king devised a plan to slow down the population growth of the Jewish nation. This plan was to eliminate all of the males born into the Israelite families. His first attempt through the hands of the midwives failed. Taking matters into his own hands, he resorted to a horrific tactic of throwing all of the newborn males into the Nile River.

It is during this period that one particular woman conceived and birthed a son, and like many, hid him for as long as she could. When it became nearly impossible to keep him from being discovered and killed, she devised a plan to make a basket that would float in water, and she placed him in the river. You might recognize this as the beginning of the life of Moses.

The king's daughter discovered Moses in the river and took him home to raise as her own. Moses grew up in the king's palace as part of his family until he made a mistake that revealed his identity. He was forced to flee to the desert for safety.

Soldiers Float

Soon, Moses would become the appointed leader to return to Egypt and deliver the Jewish nation from the oppression of Pharaoh. This wasn't an easy task as Pharaoh would agree to allow them to leave and then change his mind several times. It eventually took the death of Pharaoh's son to pave the way for Moses and the Israelite nation to leave Egypt. Even then, the Pharaoh did not give up. He sent an army to capture them and bring them back only to see his soldiers perish in the waters of the Red Sea.

The Journey Begins

Now what? Moses had the charge of leading this nation of people to the place God had promised Abraham. Along the way, there were doubts, distractions, and disobedience. Due to their rebellion, they would roam the desert for forty years before entering the Promised Land. Even then, because of his own disobedience, Moses was denied access.

Throughout his leadership journey, Moses understood a key principle: There is no success without a successor. Early in his leadership, he began to pour his life into a young leader who would assume the key leadership role after his death. This young leader was Joshua.

A New Strategy

Joshua's story is a great study in transitional leadership. He picked up right where Moses left off with the exception that there would be no more desert travels. It was time to take the land; time to move forward with purpose and passion. But that was a lot easier said than done. This new journey would require great faith, obedience, and an unswerving commitment to God's instructions.

Reading through the book of Joshua can be a little overwhelming. It is loaded with attacks, conquests, and bloodshed - a lot of bloodshed. I'm convinced that were some of these stories ever recreated on the big screen as they unfold on the pages of Scripture, they would garner an R rating.

God blessed Joshua with victory after victory as long as he followed the battle plan as dictated by God Himself.

The word on the street was the Israelites were unstoppable, and they were. Not only did they have the ideal battle plans, they had the promise from God that He would give them every place they walked, just as He had promised Moses.

We Are Our Worst Enemy

It's baffling to consider that even with credentials like this, the Israelites would ever stray away from the plan, but it happened. Pride has a tendency to show up when people start experiencing success.

The battle with pride can require more attention and energy than the area of our success. Once we find ourselves on the upside of victory, it becomes tempting to look inward for the source of our success. Psalm 10:4 shares this truth: "In his pride the wicked does not seek him; in all his thoughts there is no room for God." Once we get to this place in our life journey, we need to be on the alert. It typically doesn't end well for the person who feels they have it all under control.

Solomon is recognized as the wisest man who ever lived. During the middle phase of his life, he penned a lot of his wisdom in the book of Proverbs. When he addressed pride, he wrote, "Pride goes before destruction, a haughty spirit before a fall. Better to be lowly in spirit and among the oppressed than to share plunder with the proud."[4]

This is what happened to the Jews. Even as they began their conquests, they began to think they didn't need God's help, much less His plan. Some would even be so bold to think they had a better plan. Every time this would happen, the battle would turn against them. Joshua would have to step back and discern where they messed up, correct it, and continue his push ahead.

Famous Last Words

As the Israelites neared their final destination, Joshua was beginning to show his age. We can only imagine the effects of leading this crusade could have had on his mind and body. It was time to step down. In his parting words, we find this charge:

"The Lord has driven out before you great and powerful nations; to this day no one has been able to withstand you. One of you routs a thousand, because the Lord your God fights for you, just as he promised. So be very careful to love the Lord your God." (Joshua 23:9-11)

If I could whittle his words down, they would say: God gave success to you; you give love to God. I think that's a fair trade, don't you? But Joshua didn't stop there. He offered them a simple warning:

"But if you turn away and ally yourselves with the survivors of these nations that remain among you...then you may be sure that the Lord your God will no longer drive out these nations before you. Instead, they will become snares and traps for you, whips on your backs and thorns in your eyes, until you perish from this good land, which the Lord your God has given you." (Joshua 23:12,13)

Joshua simply advised them to "dance with the one who brung ya'!" He was clearly communicating that if they abandoned their devotion to God and His plan, they would be forfeiting His protection. That is exactly what happened.

Enemies Among Us

It didn't take long after Joshua died for the Israelites to abandon the resolve they had to obey God. Not only that, they began to adopt the evil practices and idol worship of the cities they were attacking. Time and time again, when you read this account, you see the phrase, "The Israelites did evil in the eyes of the Lord." As you might imagine, this did not set well with God.

God remained true to the promise. He removed the barrier of protection He had placed around the nation of Israel. The unbeatable were now in the Loser's Bracket. God allowed them to be overtaken by their enemies. The backdrop for the rest of our story is about one of these enemies: the Midianites.

"The people of Israel did what was evil in the sight of the Lord, and the Lord gave them into the hand of Midian seven years." (Judges 6:1)

We're Sorry

For seven years, they dealt with invasions from the Midianites, Amalakites, and other foreigners from the East. These invaders would wreak havoc on their crops, their livestock, and their people. It was seven long years of destruction and defeat.

While the Israelites had betrayed God by worshipping foreign gods, they began to cry out to the one true God for help. They were clueless as to why they were suffering so much. In His grace, God heard their cry. He sent a prophet to point out how He had brought their ancestors out of slavery and given them the land where they were dwelling only for them to betray Him by turning to foreign gods.

One Ordinary Man

God's solution to their problem was a man by the name of Gideon. He was an ordinary man whom God used in an outrageous way to show how placing all of our trust in Him enables us to do amazing things. Gideon's story reveals some very relevant attributes about our lives that we must realize if we want to see God use the life He's given to us. You are about to discover some practical steps you can take in your own life to position yourself to witness God do some OUTRAGEOUS things. You will also meet some people who have personally experienced God's work in and through their lives, people like you and me. Their stories will reveal that God is still doing the outrageous with the ordinary.

CHAPTER 2: GOD IS WITH YOU

A Letter, A Phone Call, and the Governor

I have a very active family. It's not that my wife and I sat down and developed a 5, 10 and 15-year plan to be running around chasing our kids. We just choose to be an active part of whatever develops their God-given unique gifts and abilities. One such event was a leadership development program that majored on academics and community service. It involved girls all across the state of South Carolina.

One fall, we were fortunate to serve as host for the participants in the program. My wife had the great idea that a letter of encouragement from our female governor would be a nice touch. She reached out to the Governor's office for some help.

The response was very positive. The information she received was that the Governor was excited to be a small part and would draft a letter right away. So we waited...and waited.

A few weeks went by, and Angela decided time was

running out, and a follow-up call was necessary. When she called, no one answered. She did, however, have the option to leave a message on a recording, so she left word that we needed to prepare for the event and asked if someone would return the call to update her on the status of the letter. As with most women, all of this was going on while she was handling four other tasks.

On her "to-do" list for the day was a stop at the local pet store for some food and other items. As she gathered what she needed and waited in line, her phone rang. You guessed it: the Governor's office was calling. Taking a call from our state capital in a pet store didn't seem to be the wise thing to do, but due to the nature of the call and the critical timing of it all, she took the call while waiting to check out.

Now I have to make sure you know this about my wife. She's one of those "never meets a stranger" kinds of people. She is blessed with the ability to connect with just about anyone. We call it colliding with others. And while she's doing this, she builds such rapport that an outsider might think she's talking with a friend of 20 years.

As she continued to checkout, she noticed that the gal behind the register began to go out of her way to help get her items bagged. She even offered to have someone carry them out to the car. She noted that she had never had that kind of attention before, but she moved on.

Later that night, we were going over our individual responsibilities for the event, and she shared that we would have the letter from the governor by the end of the week. Then, after a long pause, she randomly busted out laughing. Once I got her settled down, she relayed the experience I just shared, but with one additional component.

While she was on the phone at the pet store, she moved up in the line to check out, all the while talking to her new "best friend." As they were going over the details of getting the letter, Angela made this statement: "I know you guys are busy, but I need that letter from the governor in my hands by the end of the week." This explains the sudden upgrade in customer service she had received at the pet store. I guess they figured, *If this lady has this much pull with the governor, then we want to make sure she has the best experience possible.*

The point of the story is this: When you know you have great power, you can do great things. This is where Gideon found himself.

Let's Meet Gideon

Gideon was an interesting fellow. Here you have someone fully trained as a warrior, and yet we first meet him hiding in a winepress, threshing grain to avoid getting noticed by his enemy. He was quite intimidated by the Midianites, much like a little boy on the playground he shares with the class bully. He figured if he would lie low and not draw attention to himself, he would be fine. He wouldn't bother them, and they wouldn't bother him, but he always made sure he knew where they were.

As much as he attempted to be invisible, he was noticed, but not by the Midianites. The attention on this day would be from an ally, not the enemy.

You Are the Man!

As Gideon was working away, an angel appeared with a rather surprising greeting: "The Lord is with you, mighty warrior"[1], to which Gideon responded unlike so many we read about who had encounters with angels. In most accounts of angels appearing to humans, the immediate response was falling straight to the ground with fear and trembling. I must note that most theologians believe this angel was actually Jesus in His Heavenly form. Later in the text, he is identified not as "the angel of the Lord," but simply as "the Lord." And yet, standing face-to-face with the Creator of the universe, Gideon doesn't appear to flinch. In fact, he launches into a rebuttal of sorts:

"Pardon me, my lord," Gideon replied, "but if the Lord is with us, why has all this happened to us? Where are all his wonders that our ancestors told us about when they said, 'Did not the Lord bring us up out of Egypt?' But now the Lord has abandoned us and given us into the hand of Midian." (Judges 6:13)

Not quite the response I would have expected from someone so timid that they were trying not to get noticed by their enemy. I'm not sure if picking a fight with Jesus Christ would qualify as notable quality for the one of the gentlemen on "The Bachelor."

As we begin to connect the components of Gideon's life to our own, I want to submit the first component of this story: God Is with YOU!

Where's This God I've Heard About?

I find it interesting that Gideon's response was laced with his understanding of the promises of God. It is clear that he had some understanding of who God was and what He had promised his ancestors who came before him. He had heard how God worked wonders for them as they left Egypt headed to the Promised Land. Now, standing in a winepress, hiding from his enemies, and being told that "God was with him," he expressed questions that indicate he wanted to know more about

God and His plan for the Israelites.

What's your understanding of who God is and His plan for your life?

How God Sees Me

I sense that many people have very little understanding of a personal God – someone who desires to engage us and be an influence in all that we do. Let's first establish that God clearly sees us, warts and all.

"You are the God who sees me," for she said, "I have now seen the One who sees me." (Genesis 16:13)

God is a personal God who desires not only to watch us, but also unfold His purpose for our lives. The Psalmist said it simplest:

"Your eyes saw my unformed body; all the days ordained for me were written in your book before one of them came to be." (Psalm 139:1)

The Bible says we are God's "handiwork."[2] Not only that, we are a "new creation" when we place our trust in Him.[3] We are made perfect by His power and grace. It is vital to take hold of these principles because when I can see myself as God sees me, then I will live with more confidence and do as He says.

If you're a parent, you get this. How many times have you been outside with your kids while they play on the swing-set or at a pool and heard, "Watch me, Daddy" or "Mommy, look at me"? Just as our kids want our attention to show us what they can do, we long for God's attention. We long to know He's looking in our direction.

We especially want to know He see us when life gives us challenges. It is comforting to know He is watching over our lives to provide and protect.

"I will be glad and rejoice in your love, for you saw my affliction

and knew the anguish of my soul. You have not given me into the hands of the enemy but have set my feet in a spacious place." (Psalm 31:7,8)

The bottom line is that God sees us because He desires to have a personal relationship with us. Not in a mere platonic way so that we can wear the label of a Christian. His desire is that we long to spend time with Him, talk with Him, and trust Him for the outcomes in our lives. And yet, this is sometimes hindered by the limited view we have of ourselves.

I find it very encouraging that God saw Gideon's potential. I love how David Jeremiah phrases this concept when he shares, "God didn't see Gideon as he was, but as what he would become."[4] We know this because He addresses him as a "valiant warrior." This encourages me because I have confidence that He sees my potential as well. And He stirs that potential within my spirit and has all of the necessary power to help me realize that potential.

How I See Me

I've heard it said that how we identify ourselves will determine our approach to life. It's sort of like the adage that if we always carry around a hammer, then every problem looks like a nail. We need to have a healthy perspective of who we are. We need to be sure we're not allowing our lives to be defined by unhealthy influences. Here's a brief list of the most prominent ones: achievement, wealth, social acceptance, and charity.

It all comes down to priorities - those things we value most in our lives. An easy test to determine the priorities in your life is Reggie Campbell's "Obituary Test."[5]

This will take you a little time, but it is well worth the

investment. Sit down with paper and pen or a computer and write out your obituary. You may want to find a few examples to guide you. As you begin to compose the words that will be posted for the entire world to read, be sure to include quotes from your spouse, your parents, your children, your employer, and your closest friends. The components of life you want them to use to reflect who you "were" are the things you assign the greatest value.

Similarly, how we identify what is most important to us is an expression of how we see ourselves. And if the life we are living in the present is not consistent with the life we want at the end, we tend to ask, "What am I going to do to develop these attributes?" That is a very dangerous path to follow. If I find my value in what I do, then I'll always have to do more to determine my value to others. Rather than look for my value in what I do, I need to base it on something greater than my human limitations. Our value and our priorities should be birthed out of a personal relationship with Jesus Christ.

How I See God

God wants us to look for Him. He knows that if we do, we will find Him. Proverbs 7:15 reveals, "So I came out to meet you; I looked for you and have found you!"

A recent survey by the Barna Group shares that 83% of Americans consider themselves to be Christians.[6] What would make this study a little more interesting would be to find out how this 83% became Christians. This would reflect how they see God. Based on my experience, there are three paths that most people cite as their path to God.

"My parents are Christians." This is Christianity by genetics. Some look at their relationship with God as

something that was passed down from their parents as an inheritance. The challenge with this perspective is that we allow our parents to define who God is to us. If this is the case, then He is limited to mere human description and abilities.

"We're Americans; we're all Christians. We just need to make sure our good outweighs our bad." This is Christianity by geography. Some see God as a universal being who wants everyone to get along on Earth and eventually come to Heaven and hang out with Him. They just need to make sure the "Good Deed Account" has more than the "Mistake Account."

While being a good person is a quality to strive for, it does very little to qualify us for a place of perfection like Heaven. In fact, if you take imperfect people into a perfect environment, the perfect environment is no longer perfect. One of the two must change. For the sake of eternity, Heaven isn't going to change. C.S. Lewis posed it this way: "Heaven is reality itself. All that is fully real is Heavenly. For all that can be shaken will be shaken and only the unshakeable remains."[7] The person striving to be "good enough" will not fare too well because "good enough" has to be perfection.

"My sin separates me from God. I must accept the sacrifice of Jesus as the only way to be a Christian." This is Christianity by grace. The Bible teaches there is only one way for people to be a part of God's family. There must be a pivotal time in our lives where we come to understand our imperfection as humans separates us from Him. That's why He provided the means to Himself through the sacrifice of Jesus Christ. Jesus dying on the cross is not just a story; it's the bridge that allows us access to God. When we discover this truth and choose to cross this

bridge by faith, we begin a personal relationship with our Heavenly Father.

That's how God wants us to see Him; as a Heavenly Father who longs for a personal relationship with us. Not just any relationship, but one that empowers us to do great things. I fear many people fail to realize or consider that they have more potential than they think. Too often we put limitations on our own lives. God has so much He wants to do in and through us, but we constantly stiff-arm Him to keep Him at a safe distance. With the confidence that God is with us just as He was with Gideon, we must break through the limitations we place on ourselves.

"The Lord Is With You"…Again

The first message the angel shared was, "The Lord is with you." What does it mean to you to know that the Lord is with YOU? It's an interesting observation to learn the phrase; "The Lord is with you" is used only three other times in the NIV Bible. Let's take a look at these occurrences and what we can glean from their use.

"The Lord Is With You" is Affirming.

The next reference surfaces when King Solomon realizes the Arc of the Covenant that served as the dwelling place for God's presence was housed in a tent while he looked on from the window of his palace. He commits to building a permanent structure for God's dwelling place. The prophet Nathan encourages Solomon with, "Whatever you have in mind, go ahead and do it, for the Lord is with you."[8] Solomon made a very good decision and the prophet Nathan was affirming his decision.

"The Lord Is With You" is Dependent.

The next occurrence is once again used as a form of encouragement. In 2 Chronicles 14, we read the story of King Asa's victory in a battle where he was grossly outnumbered. The key to his success was the simple prayer he prayed just before the battle:

"Lord, there is no one like you to help the powerless against the mighty. Help us, Lord our God, for we rely on you, and in your name we have come against this vast army. Lord, you are our God; do not let mere mortals prevail against you." (2 Chronicles 14:11)

On the heels of this victory where God pretty much did it all, King Asa is greeted by the prophet Azariah with this simple word:

"The Lord is with you when you are with him. If you seek him, he will be found by you, but if you forsake him, he will forsake you." (2 Chronicles 15:2)

As the late Jimmy Valvano, the late NC State basketball coach would say often, "Don't mess with the happy." Azariah was conveying a simple message: If life is good, don't change it. The Lord is with you as long as you are with Him.

"The Lord Is With You" is Empowering.

The final utterance of this phrase falls on the ears of a young girl who is terrified and confused. She's having a face-to-face with an angel who greets her with, "Greetings, you who are highly favored! The Lord is with you."[9] This young girl is Mary, the mother of Jesus. The angel goes on to unfold the plan that would be the turning point for all of mankind. In the face of confusion, uncertainty, and opportunity, knowing the Lord is with you is very empowering. When you don't know where to turn, you can start with Him.

The bottom line is that the outrageous life begins with knowing the Lord and living with the understanding that He is with you and that you are not alone. When we truly understand this principle, we tap into something that will help us do the outrageous. We just need to remember that we have an active part to play.

the OUTRAGEOUS life

CHAPTER 3: MY CONTRIBUTION IS CRITICAL

As the story continues, Gideon is obviously confused. On one hand, he's heard about the greatness of God and the many miracles He leveraged for the good of the Israelites, all the while cowering from the Midianites to avoid harassment and possibly an attack. I'm sure you can see why the assurance from Jesus that He was with him was critical.

What the Lord says next probably took Gideon to a place he was not expecting:

"The Lord turned to him and said, "Go in the strength you have and save Israel out of Midian's hand. Am I not sending you?" (Judges 6:14)

I can almost hear it now: "Do what?"

God wanted to rescue His chosen nation, and, as is His pattern throughout Scripture, He chooses to use the most unlikely of people. These were individuals who were minding their own business, just making it day by day. And yet God knew their potential and wanted to use them to accomplish something great for His Kingdom.

When you think about God using you for something great, what comes to mind? Do you think, "Do what?" or does that notion get you a little excited? Do you think, "What could I possibly offer to God that He could use for helping others transfer their trust over to Him?"

I think this is the first dead-end we hit when we begin thinking about seeing God's work manifested in our lives. We disqualify ourselves right off the bat because we filter the opportunities through the lens of how "little" we have to offer. Jesus provided a great word to Gideon that we all need to establish in our minds: "Go in the strength you have." When we think about the work of God in and through our lives, we must know that our contribution is critical.

Instead of focusing on all of the things you can't do, why not consider what you can do? Going through Scripture, you can discover many people who pushed back from an opportunity to be used by God with the excuse of "What could I possibly have that God could use?" When Moses attempted to get out of his call to lead the Israelites out of Egypt, God asked him, "What's that in your hand?" David responded to the challenge of fighting a giant with just a sling and a stone. Do you recall the woman who washed the feet of Jesus with perfume and her hair as a form of worship? While each of these and many more like them never saw where they were headed, they were willing to use what they had so that God could do something great.

When I consider this notion in the context of people I know, none rings louder in my mind than Wallace Nix from Chosen Children Ministries.

Orphans and More

Chosen Children Ministries (CCM) began as a vision to rescue orphaned children in Nicaragua. When Wallace and his wife, Kim, came on board as directors, they had no idea where God was going to take them and CCM. Not long after they began serving, God impressed upon them a strategy of using the platform of CCM to spread the Gospel beyond the orphanage and into the barrios that were spread all over the country. A barrio is a Hispanic neighborhood of low-income to poverty-stricken families. The desire to share the love of Jesus Christ with these folks birthed a vision to begin planting churches and staffing them with pastors who would serve, teach, and lead.

In addition to serving the people of Nicaragua, CCM provided the vehicle for Americans to visit and join them in their labor one week at a time. Wallace and Kim would use these human resources to canvas neighborhoods, conduct Vacation Bible Schools for children, teach adult Bible studies and build homes and churches. The vision quickly grew beyond the 20 or so children in the CCM orphanage. In fact, it grew faster than they were prepared to grow.

No Room in the Inn

The telling moment was when a church called to ask if they could bring 88 teenagers and adults. If they could pull it off, it would be the largest group they had ever hosted. Up to this point, the most they could house was 40 people, so to commit to 48 more without a sure place to lay their heads was a huge step of faith. Wallace had a decision to make: turn them away because he did not have accommodations for a group of that size or say

"Yes" and figure out how to make it work. The problem was they had no idea how they were going to do that.

The obvious action was to build a second dormitory. The problem was they only had $1200.00 to spend. Not 100% sure of construction costs in Nicaragua, Wallace had his director find out how far the $1200.00 would go. The answer came back that they could begin building the foundation for a new dorm, but that was as far as the money would take them. In fact, it would only cover materials and not the labor. The question from the staff was, "What now?" Wallace's response was simple: "Let's do what we can with what we have." So, with shovels in hand, Wallace and the CCM staff began digging the footings for the foundation.

When a Stranger Calls

One morning after beginning this process, Wallace's cell phone rang. He took the call to hear the voice of a lady in America asking for a few minutes of his time. She began to share how her family wanted to help Chosen Children in some way. She asked, "What do you need?" This is a common question for the Nixes, so they tend to be ready with appeals for help with the orphanage.

"We have some of our children who need to be sponsored," Wallace shared. She laughed and said, "Surely there's something else." Looking up from his hole in the ground, Wallace saw the bus they used to transport their guests and shared, "Our bus could use some new tires." She laughed again and pressed him with, "What else do you need?"

By now the work-break was getting old, as was the notion of throwing out a laundry list, until he shared something with which she connected. Wallace suggested,

"How about you telling me how much you want to help and I'll find the matching item?" Her response caught him off-guard. "What are you doing right now that only God can finish?"

Without missing a second, Wallace replied, "Right now I am standing in a ditch. We are digging footings for a dormitory to house 48 high school students this summer. All we have is $1200.00, and we're trusting God to provide the rest of the money we need to finish the project." Her response? "Build it, and build it the way you want it, and I'll pay for it."

Our contribution is critical. When faced with opportunities to do something great for God, we must never underestimate the part we play in His work. We just have to use what we have and leave the results to Him.

What is it that you would love to do but keep excusing away? It's the subject of the silent conversation you have with yourself quite often. You say to yourself, "I would love to ____", but it never gets any traction. Why is that? Chances are, it's because you tell yourself all the reasons it would fail before you ever consider the reasons why it would succeed. It's an inner battle that must be won.

The Inner Battle

In our family, fall isn't as much football season as it is cross-country season. In case you're not familiar, that's running 3.1 miles (5K) over a variety of terrain. I am thrilled that my kids are committed to this sport. It's something they can do for the rest of their lives, and the experiences they are having are molding them into very disciplined individuals. The discipline to compete in this sport requires a lot of inner battles we like to call "You vs. You."

A friend of ours recently shared this poem:

THE RUNNER'S PRAYER
Lord, watch over me today as I run.
This is the day and this is the time for the race.
Watch over my body.
Keep it free from injury.
Watch over my mind.
Watch over my spirit.
Watch over my competitors.
Remind us that we are struggling equally.
Lord, let me win.
Not by coming in ahead of my friends, but by beating myself.
A battle won over me.
And may I say at the end,
"I have fought a good fight.
I have finished the race.
I have kept the faith."
- Author Unknown

This is the essential battle that must be won, not just in running, but in life. And just like in running, our opponent is not another person; it's ourselves.

Moving Past My Limits

In my own life, I find there are things I would love to accomplish, but I do nothing toward seeing them come to fruition. Why is that? Sometimes it's because I convince myself that they will just one day magically unfold before my eyes. I need a better strategy than that. Here are four ways to getting past your limits:

1) Filter Your Plans Through God's Plan.

Jeremiah 29:11 makes it clear that God has a plan for us to follow: "'For I know the plans I have for you,'" declares the LORD, 'plans to prosper you and not to harm you, plans to give you hope and a future.'" The challenge for us is to allow Him to mold these hopes, dreams, and desires within our hearts. Proverbs 16:3 reveals, "Commit to the LORD whatever you do, and he will establish your plans."

Here's a simple strategy to keep your plans centered on God's P.L.A.N.:

Pray: Prayer is the vehicle by which we align our lives with the things of God. Our prayers may not always change our circumstances, but they do change us. When prayer is the foundation of our lives and not an accessory, we find that we are more in sync. It's like plugging my "iProduct" into my computer and clicking on "Sync." It makes sure that the product of choice is current with any changes or updates. That's what prayer does for our plans.

Listen - Scripture and Silence: God wants to communicate with us. I fear that we forget He made us to fellowship with Him. But there's not much fellowship if we're doing all of the talking. There needs to be time in our day when we are looking for and listening to Him. Jeremiah 29:13 says it best: "You will seek me and find me when you seek me with all your heart." In our attempt to make sure our plans are part of His plans, we must seek Him through the pages of His Word and build in time to simply listen in silence. While He can reveal himself however He chooses, I believe He doesn't want to compete with all the "noise" we build into our lives. Just like the Psalmist shares, "Be still, and know that I am God…" (Psalm 46:10)

Allow Time: Waiting is never easy, that is, if you're doing nothing. Allowing time for God to respond does not have to be a drudgery. It can actually be an exciting time in your life. As you wait, your goal should be to actively look for what God is doing.

For years, I have felt like I had a book in me - not so much a topic that needed to be shared, but just the notion of committing my time and energy to putting ideas on paper in the form of a book. When I finally dispelled all of the excuses, I entered into this period of waiting. I was ready, but I didn't want to write something for the sake of writing. I knew that this commitment had to be fueled by more than a "good idea." I committed to the process, but waited on God to give me the content.

As I waited, I would filter many things through the lens of, "Is this what I'm supposed to write about?" I was constantly looking for content that might be used to create a book, but never writing. Just waiting...

The interesting thing about allowing time for God to respond is that you never know when or how He will move. For me, the idea for this book came to me while I was at a summer camp where I was speaking. It was as if the Lord said, "Okay, it's time to write a book." In the next 15 minutes, I had the Scriptural background (Gideon), ten chapter titles, and key content for each one.

Notify Trusted Friends: God never intended for us to do life alone. All through Scripture, we find men and women doing great things for God, and, more often than not, other people accompany them. When it comes to lining up with God's plan for our lives, we need others praying for us, encouraging us, and holding us accountable. We need to let our closest, most trusted friends know what God is doing so they can be a part of the process and lend a hand.

2) Write out your hopes, dreams and desires.

I am a firm believer of putting goals and dreams on paper. Studies have shown that when we write things down, we are much more likely to see them completed. But we don't need a study to prove this notion. It's just common sense, and it's modeled in the Bible.

Daniel is most commonly known for his sleep-over in the lion's den because he was caught praying to his God instead of the king's god. His story is not just about one man's devotion to his God but about a very influential man's devotion to his God. Daniel was a very high-ranking official. He had earned that spot because he could interpret the king's dreams.

The thing I noticed about Daniel's dream-casting ability is that "he wrote down the dream" (Daniel 7:1-3). Obviously Daniel had not read the studies on writing down your hopes, dreams and desires, but he understood that he needed to capture what was in his mind and put it down on paper. The old adage just makes sense: Out of sight, out of mind.

The times in my life where I see the most progress are the times when I make a list of what needs to get done or what I am working toward, and I keep that list where I can see it every day. As you feel God has placed a desire to do something greater than your perceived ability, write it down and pray over it every time you see it.

The people I see getting things done are the people with a list. The former football coach, Lou Holtz is known for his list of 107 goals he wrote out one day while unemployed. He proudly showed his wife this list, hoping to receive affirmation for desiring to accomplish so much. After looking over the list, she said, "You forgot one." Thinking she had caught on to the vision, Lou asked,

"Oh, what should I add?" Only to hear his wife reply, "Get a job."

3) Use what you have.

I'm challenging you to find your strengths. What skills do you have that set you apart? What problems do others consistently ask you to help them solve? You have to determine what this is and drill down.

I think of Moses in the Bible and how God wanted him to lead the Israelites out of Egypt. God recognized that Moses had limitations, but he also had strengths. He didn't allow what Moses could not do to keep him from where he added the most value. To compensate for his weakness, God surrounded Moses with people to make up the difference, in particular, his brother Aaron. When Moses fell short in communicating with Pharaoh, Aaron became the "Press Secretary."

The key for us is to simply use what we have for the glory of God. In other words, do what we can with what we have and leave the results to Him. Just like Peter did in Luke 5, we have to "let down our nets" and let God bring the fish. I have seen in my own life areas where I try to create results, only to see things fall apart. It is when I give my attention only to what I can do and not the results that growth and forward progress begin to take place.

There is a tendency to identify our weaknesses and drill down on them to improve in those areas. But as John Maxwell challenges people, you're only going to improve by a small margin. If you're a "4" at a particular task and you work hard, you might get it up to a "6." All the while, you are missing out on completing a task that needs your giftedness at a "9" or "10." Do what you do best, and delegate the rest.

4) Know where you are.

There's an ongoing discussion in our home about getting lost. My wife contends that a person is lost the moment they do a U-turn. The notion that you aren't sure where you are earns you the label of being lost. I would submit that as long as you know where you are, you're not lost. Just because I'm not where I want to be at the moment does not justify a "Search and Rescue" mission.

Part of the success journey is to keep tabs on your progress or lack thereof. Just like a coach must make adjustments to his game plan based on the score, we have to make adjustments in order to keep moving toward our goals. "Knowing where you are" helps you to keep the goal in front of you and part of your daily thinking and praying.

Winners are Losers

The greatest challenge for all of us is to not be our greatest opponent. We all fight the battle of "You vs. You," and we must be the winner and not the loser. The good news is that we don't have to fight it alone. God wants to see our lives count for good. In fact, He wants it to count for His glory. He expects that and will hold us accountable for the life He's given us. We can't afford to waste it...it's the only one we have. Don't allow self-imposed limitations to keep you from fulfilling your potential.

CHAPTER 4: MY OBSTACLES ARE HIS OPPORTUNITIES

Our family recently made the trek to Orlando, Florida to visit the parks at Walt Disney World. The day we visited Animal Kingdom provided us with a shorter day since the park closes earlier than the others. We ended up in a quaint little sandwich shop surrounded by locals getting together for dinner. Due to the size of the room, there wasn't a lot of space between tables.

As we sat there eating, my 8-year-old son pulled his mom over to whisper something in her ear. Her reaction was very intriguing because she almost choked on her food trying to contain her laughter. She was trying not to draw attention to herself but was having a difficult time.

To make matters worse, she wouldn't tell me what he said. She refused to say anything until we left the sandwich shop. Once we got to the car, she started laughing again and finally shared the object of her uncontrollable laughter.

Avery said, "Mom, the people next to us must be on a

date because the man keeps talking about himself…(pause)…and married people don't do that."

The perspective of a child can be very revealing and humbling. It's how they see life that makes them so much fun. That's the joy and the curse of perspectives. How we see life and its opportunities and challenges will determine the impact they will have on our lives. Your perspective will either compel you to be better or it will skew how you see the circumstances in your life and all the bad things that can happen.

Gideon: The Master of Excuses

As Gideon stood there having his face-to-face with God, he began to consider what he was being charged to do. The task placed before him was beginning to come into focus, and he didn't like what he saw. Judges 6:15 reads, "Pardon me, my lord," Gideon replied, "but how can I save Israel? My clan is the weakest in Manasseh, and I am the least in my family."

When challenged with the opportunity to do something great, all Gideon saw was limitations, obstacles and problems. He was about to miss out on the opportunity for God to use his life for something truly outrageous. He only saw all the reasons he could not do what God was asking and never considered that with God's help, it could be done.

Are you an excuse-maker?

Even the Great Ones Have Excuses

For four years, Michelangelo mounted a curved, stepped scaffold of his own design in the Vatican and went to work on the ceiling 50 feet above the floor of the Sistine Chapel. It was not his favorite thing to do. "My brush is above my head and drips paint on my face," he wrote. "I am bent like a bow and my back aches. Dear friend, rescue me now. I am not in a good place. And I am no painter."[1]

We all have challenges and problems to solve

I once heard that the people who don't have problems live in the graveyard. Everybody has problems. If this is true, then the only difference is how we see those problems. It's all about perspective.

Let's establish a consensus definition of perspective. A perspective is a mental view or outlook.[2] It's how you filter information and what you do with that information. We all see things differently. Some see the best while others see the worst.

My favorite story about perspective involves a father and his two little sons, one of whom was an eternal optimist, while the other was a perpetual pessimist. One Christmas, he decided to try to temper both of their perspectives – in addition to their standard gifts, he told them they'd each get something "chosen especially for you!" His plan was to give the pessimist every toy and game he could possibly desire, while the optimist would be directed to the basement filled with manure.

On Christmas, after the normal presents were opened, the father sent the optimist to the cellar, while leading the pessimist to the room filled with presents. After the pessimist opened all the gifts, he turned to his father with a sad face and said, "How can I possibly use all these? The TV will wear out, the PlayStation will get smashed, and all the other toys will be broken!"

After a few minutes of listening to such woe, the father remembered his optimistic son and ran to the basement steps. There in the basement was his other son, swimming through the manure with a gleeful smile. The father asked him why he was so happy, to which the boy exclaimed, "With this much manure, there must be a pony in here somewhere!"[3]

Problems As Opportunities

The challenge for us is to not give way to our immediate, man-made reaction to panic but to recognize our obstacles as opportunities. The outrageous life really is a matter of perspective.

Have you ever considered the notion that our challenges are God's opportunity to show off? Typically, the bigger the obstacle, the greater the potential to see something great happen in your life. Consider these scenarios we find in the pages of Scripture:

- The first city the Israelites encounter on the conquest of the Promised Land was Jericho. Instead of giving them a straight up battle plan, God directs them to march in circles and watch the walls fall down.

- The disciples were caught paddling a boat in a storm, and Peter gets to hydroplane across the top of the water.

- Mary and Martha's brother dies while Jesus purposely delays his arrival only to show up and show out by raising Lazarus from the dead.

In each of these instances and many more like them, the surface circumstances seemed dim. But when God interjected His power, they turned bright. They became outrageous opportunities. Not to mention how He changed the lives of the people involved. At the time, all they saw was a wall of obstacles. That's how it is with us.

It would be very helpful if we could have a GPS for our lives and could see where our circumstances are taking us.

Wish We Could See the Plan

There's a great line in the movie, *The Adjustment Bureau*, starring Matt Damon. His character is a congressman whose life is being directed and redirected by so-called agents who resemble angels executing some divine plan. Their task is to keep him on a predetermined plan that was crafted by a supreme power they recognize as the "Chairman."

After a bout with the congressman's attempt to thwart the plan, two agents are shown looking out of a high-rise window over the city below as one questions if the plan is always right.

Harry Mitchell: You ever wonder, if it's right? I mean, if it's always right?

Richardson: Not like I used to. Look, the Chairman has the plan; we only see part of it.[4]

This is how we experience life. We only see part of it, while God sees the big picture. He knows how the challenges in our lives will shape and mold us into the person He created us to be.

Is Cancer a Good Gift?

The real test comes when we are face to face with challenging circumstances, and we have a choice to make with our reactions: Do we panic and see no further than the obstacle in front of us; or do we pause long enough to realize that God really is in control, and whatever has birthed fear and uncertainty in our lives is part of what He's doing for our good?

Zac Smith was faced with such a scenario. Diagnosed

with Stage Four Colon Cancer, he had a choice to make about the obstacle in his life. Instead of stringing you along, I'll share with you that he won his battle with cancer by stepping out of his body here on Earth into the presence of the One who created his body and the cancer that took his life.

Zac was a healthy thirty-two year old with a beautiful wife, three children, a home, and a job he loved. When doctors removed the lemon-sized tumor and eighteen inches of his large intestine, they discovered the cancer was spreading. Chemotherapy was next on the list.

Like most people in this scenario, Zac was confused and full of questions – not medical questions, but life questions. Questions like: Why do I have cancer? Had I done something wrong? Was this the result of many years of past sin? Where did I go wrong?

Believe it or not, there is good news in times such as this. As a Christian, Zac had hope – hope in something far greater than doctors or chemotherapy. His hope was in Jesus Christ. The Old Testament prophet, Jeremiah, encourages us with the truth that God has a destination for our lives.

"For I know the plans I have for you," declares the Lord, "plans to prosper you and not to harm you, plans to give you hope and a future." (Jeremiah 29:11)

While we may not understand the paths we take to get there, we must trust Him and know that He's got everything under control.

Zac's treatment began to make progress in overcoming the cancer. In fact, at one point it appeared the cancer was gone. There was a short-lived celebration as the cancer returned with a vengeance. Doctors exhausted all possible treatments, and surgery was not even an option.

Medically speaking, there was no hope for healing. Zac would be left to enjoy his life the best he could until the cancer would claim his life. But what he did up to that day was incredible. He leveraged his obstacle as a tool to honor and elevate the name of Jesus.

Zac's perspective of the cancer attacking his body was that it was a gift from God. He stood on Matthew 7:11, which teaches how God gives good things to those who ask. In other words, God cannot give you a bad gift.

In his own words, Zac shared that "cancer was the best thing that has ever happened to [him]." Cancer made him a better husband, a better father, and a better employee. Most of all, he was able to gain a perspective of God that allowed him to be a better follower of Jesus Christ.

This is the amazing part of Zac's story. His perspective on his obstacle did not open up bouts of anger and bitterness. Rather it positioned him to welcome cancer as a vehicle for God to be glorified. His strongest statement about his battle with cancer says it best:

"If God chooses to heal me, God is God and God is good. If God chooses not to heal me and allows me to die, God is God and God is still good. To God be the glory."

How Do You Respond to Obstacles?

When we face obstacles, we have choices – not just the choices involved with the obstacles, but the ultimate choice of how we are going to respond to the obstacle. How we respond will say a lot about our character and what we believe.

Make Excuses

An excuse is our way of attempting to transfer responsibility for something to anything but us. When we make excuses for something done or not done, we communicate a lot about our character. People will see that the lack of confidence we have in ourselves is greater than the amount of confidence we have in God. I tend to subscribe to the slogan I read on a T-shirt once: "Everyone has excuses, but not everyone chooses to use them." Our excuses declare the limitations we've set for our lives.

The good news is that God has no limitations. If we'll connect to Him with our hook of faith and hold on for dear life, He'll take us beyond our limits and enable us to do things we've only dreamed of doing.

When charged to go deliver his people from the Midianites, Gideon immediately saw his limitations and resorted to excuses. He isn't alone in his excuse-ridden response. All through scripture we find others who opted to avoid responsibility and transfer blame to something other than themselves.

In the Garden of Eden, God created the first man, Adam and his lovely bride, Eve. They had the easy life: relax, focus on populating the earth and eat anything you wanted except from one tree that sits in the middle of the garden. [Spoiler Alert] You guessed it, they didn't listen. So God shows up and confronts Adam. This is where we hear the very first excuse uttered from the lips of man: "The woman!" But Adam didn't stop there; he went so far as to pin his mistake on God: "…that YOU gave me."[5] Needless to say, it was all downhill from there.

Many years later, civilization is in full swing, and God's chosen nation of Israel has found itself captured as slaves in Egypt. God decides it's time to relocate, but that won't happen without a fight. He needs an advocate to intercede for the people and to lead them to a new location, the place He promised their forefathers. Moses is that leader. But instead of embracing the honor of being considered able and prepared to take on this task, all Moses can do is think of all the reasons he can't:

Excuse #1: Who am I that I should go to Pharaoh?

Excuse #2: What if they ask me who sent me?

Excuse #3: What if they don't believe me?

Excuse #4: I'm not eloquent; I can't speak well.

Excuse #5: Please send someone else.

Then the text reads, "the Lord's anger burned against Moses…"[6]

If you fast forward into the New Testament, the excuses don't stop. In fact, all throughout the Gospels, Jesus was challenging people to a higher level of living and was consistently met with excuses as to why they couldn't make that happen.

One afternoon, Jesus and his band of disciples were out in their version of a flash mob. Typically everywhere they went in public was a flash mob minus the dancing. This particular mob numbered over five thousand people.

The disciples stopped what they were doing long enough to realize they were hungry and suggested that they close up for the day and send everyone home to eat. But Jesus had a better plan – "You feed them." Immediately they checked the budget and determined rather quickly they would be stretched thin to cover that expense. "That would take more than half a year's wages! Are we to go and spend that much on bread and give it to them to eat?" (Mark 6:37)

After working past their self-imposed limitations, Jesus

performed one of His greatest miracles and fed this mob of people with just two fishes and five loaves of bread. The cool part is that when it was all over, there were twelve baskets full of leftovers – one for each disciple. No more excuses.

Fix it Ourselves

This is another instinctive response, especially for men. Men are fixers. Give a man a little time and some duct tape, and he can fix anything. But there's only so much we can do in our own ability. At best, it buys us a little time and creates short-term success. Eventually, however, life breaks again, and you're back where you started.

Thinking of fixing things reminds me of the story told about the Ohio gentleman whose oil well caught fire. He put out an all-points bulletin for assistance. To ensure a heavy response, the oil baron also offered a $30,000 reward to whoever could quench the flames. All the large firehouses from Newell, Chester, East Liverpool, Wellsville, Salineville, and Dillonvale sent help. They dispatched their best companies, accompanied by their most modern fire-fighting equipment. However, not one of their trucks could get within 200 yards of the blaze. The heat was just too intense.

Finally, the Calcutta Township Volunteer Fire Department appeared on the scene. They had only one rickety truck equipped with a single ladder, two buckets of water, three buckets of sand, and a blanket. It didn't even come with a hose. When that old truck reached the point where all those other fire companies had stopped, its driver didn't hesitate. He kept barreling ahead until he and his crew were on top of the blaze. Calcutta's volunteers leapt out of the truck, threw the two buckets of water and three buckets of sand on the inferno, then beat the fire out with the blanket.

That oil man was so impressed by this display of courage, he gave the driver $30,000 in cash on the spot and asked "What are you and your men going to do with all that money?" The driver didn't hesitate, replying, "The first thing we're going to do is get those gosh darn brakes on that truck fixed."

Let God Handle It

The best option is to let God handle our obstacles. As we see in Zac's story, this is the ultimate goal. The obstacles in our lives are not there to slow us down. Sometimes they are there to re-direct our focus and allow us to gain a new and clearer perspective of who God is and what He's capable of doing. His ultimate desire is for us to know Him more intimately and to experience His love on an entirely new level.

This can only happen when we yield more of our life to Him and desire to have more of Him and less of us in our lives. I love pastor Mark Batterson's perspective as he shared this during a recent conference: "If you don't have a hunger for the things of God, then you must be full of yourself."

In Gideon's case, that's exactly where God wanted to be. He wanted "G" not to worry about what he could do in his limited ability but to know and believe that the Lord would be with him, and, together, they would do something great. In His own words, the Lord answered, "I will be with you, and you will strike down all the Midianites, leaving none alive."[7] I can almost hear His modern day vernacular: "We got this. Trust me and watch what happens."

It is a great opportunity to be in the presence of someone who gets this principle. They are marked individuals who have been in the battles of obstacles and witnessed God's supernatural provision. They have seen the outrageous up close. You can feel their faith. You can see it in their eyes. You can hear it in their voice.

Jon Estes is one of those people.

No Clue in Cleveland, GA

Jon was a twenty-four year old young man with a business degree trying to figure out life. Through a series of events, he found himself on the campus of an old Bible Memory Association camp in Cleveland, GA with no plans, no vision, and most challenging, no money. But he did have one thing: a crystal clear direction from the Lord. As he looked around at the 132 acre, run down facility, God clearly expressed to Jon, "This will become a place where lives will be changed. It will be you or someone else, but I will build a camp here." Jon decided he would be that person.

As Jon accepted the opportunity to take the lead of what is known today as Woodlands Camp, he turned to Scripture. As he prayed over the words he read, he landed on a passage that has become the foundational verse for all he does: *"Unless the Lord builds the house, the builders labor in vain."* (Psalm 127:1)

This verse would change the way Jon prayed forever. As he accepted the call to take the helm of Woodlands Camp, Jon's foundational prayer would become, "God, will you _____?" He wanted God involved in all of the details and did not want to assume credit for anything that happened at Woodlands. Jon wanted his life to be completely in sync with where God was taking him. He wanted to be going in the same direction and at the same pace, not ahead or behind.

The World's Largest Mud Pit

Jon would take the next few years learning how to run a camp and how to keep it afloat financially. It soon became clear that they needed to grow, but they were limited based on their current facilities, which weren't very stellar. The centerpiece of the entire campus, the lake, needed attention as well. It became clear that upgrades were a necessity.

After the construction of two new cabins increased the camp capacity to 192 campers, it was determined that the lake needed a facelift. The years of rain run-off from dirt and gravel roads had lifted the bottom of the lake. Dredging would be necessary in order to get the depth to safe levels for the many lake activities campers had come to love so much. There was also the matter of constructing a new bridge.

The project would begin by draining the lake dry. But there was the matter of timing. Could they drain the lake and have it refilled before campers arrived in June? After days of research, it was determined that an oversized siphon could be constructed to quickly move the water from the lake to a nearby creek. They built a simple system of PVC pipe and turned it "on." After 10 days of nature's water pump at work, the lake sat empty. It was time to begin dredging the silt and sand from the bottom.

Removing the contents of the lake bottom turned out to be a bigger project than expected. With limited resources and machinery, clearing the bottom of the lake was going to take a lot longer than expected. Then the phone rang.

Jon had a friend who lived in nearby Atlanta and owned a commercial business that majored in heavy machinery. His workload had all but stopped due to a sudden and extreme downturn in the US economy. He had heard about Jon's project and asked, "What if I bring all of my equipment and some workers and come spend a month clearing the bottom of your lake?" They agreed on an amazing price and got to work.

The new crew arrived and quickly increased the amount of mud, sand and silt that was being pulled from the lake. In fact, the contractor offered to take on a second project, rebuilding the headwall around the swim area at no additional cost. While they finished that project, the Woodlands team conquered the new bridge. The "lake project" was going better than imagined. Soon it would be time to begin re-filling the lake.

As with many lakes, the Woodlands Lake was fed by underground springs and rain. There was no accurate method to determine how much water would be coming into the lake each day. Not knowing this information created a somewhat stressful situation. What compounded things even more was the matter of a severe two-year drought across the entire Southeast.[8] There were restrictions on water use as lake levels all around reached dangerously low levels.

As they watched and waited patiently for the lake to begin filling up, time was of the essence. It was March, and campers would be arriving in two months. At the given rate of water coming in, they were seven feet short of being completely refilled.

You can imagine the burden Jon and his staff carried each day as they watched and waited for the water to rise.

Not just the burden, but the mere fact that the centerpiece of the camp was non-existent was a very big concern. If there was no lake, it was hard to imagine what a day at camp would look like. Could they even hold camp without a lake? This was enough to drive a person to their knees in prayer.

If you recall Jon's filter for how he would lead at Woodlands, you will remember his heavy dependence on God to build the camp. As he prayed for water, he began to sense God directing him to ask others to join him. They created an initiative they would call the "Pray for Rain Campaign." The Woodlands staff began using every means of contact and communication they could to ask people to pray for rain. Guess what happened: it started to rain.

And it didn't stop raining. Jon went and found a tape measure and began making daily trips to a spot on the lake to measure the increase. Each day they would post a photo on Facebook to show those who were praying how the obstacle they were facing was God's opportunity to show off. After two months of praying and raining, the lake was just twelve inches short of being completely filled up.

Jon realized the true work of God one morning as he watched the news while getting ready for the day. The news anchor made a comment to the effect of, "Spring 2009 will go down in the record books as the rainiest spring in the last 100 years." What a dichotomy: the rainiest spring in the middle of a severe drought. That's outrageous! You go God!

The question is not, "Will we have problems?" but, "Will the problems have us?" It's all a matter of perspective. Jon didn't see an empty lake. He saw an opportunity for God to do what only God could do. The challenge is for us is to get out of His way.

As I am around individuals who are striving to stay out of God's way, I see them accomplishing things they never dreamed or saw coming. I'm beginning to think that it's not the size of the dream as much as it is the size of the dream-maker. If you are the dream-maker, then don't expect great things to happen. But if God is the originator of your dreams, you should be a little intimidated. If we can create the plan and strategy, then we're just getting in the way. It's like Jeff Goins says in his book, *Wrecked*, "What if the purpose of my life is not about me? Am I willing to give up all my dreams...to find it?"[9]

Obstacles aren't always in our way to keep us from doing something. They might just be there to show us and others how great and powerful God really is. After all, He's not surprised. In fact, it could be that He sometimes stacks the cards against Himself just so we can be reminded of what He's capable of doing. When you find yourself facing challenges, don't see them as being in the way. Consider them to be opportunities for God to do a great work, and begin looking for the outrageous ending to unfold in the moment that you least expect.

CHAPTER 5: SMALL BATTLES, BIG VICTORIES

Let's hit "Refresh" for a moment and recap where Gideon has been and where he is going. We discovered Gideon hiding from the Amalekites in a winepress while threshing wheat. His intention was to not draw any attention to himself and avoid getting noticed by his enemies. He was not very successful as God shows up and calls him out for what he really is, a warrior. This is not quite the label you assign to someone hiding out in a winepress.

God begins to lay out a plan to rescue his children, the Israelites, from being terrorized by these foreigners. There's just one catch...He's appointed Gideon as the leader of this revolt. Naturally Gideon pushes back with all kinds of excuses. He doesn't see what could be, but rather, what can't be. Gideon's perspective is about to hold him back from something amazing – something outrageous.

Truth or Dare, Level 1

In this moment of doubt, Gideon comes up with an idea to find out if God is serious about this whole "Go Save Israel" initiative. He decides to put God to a test. What he doesn't know is he's the one about to be tested. Let's look in on the conversation:

"Gideon replied, 'If now I have found favor in your eyes, give me a sign that it is really you talking to me. Please do not go away until I come back and bring my offering and set it before you.' And the Lord said, 'I will wait until you return.'" (Judges 6:17, 18)

Gideon goes away and prepares a ceremonial meal for God. When he returns, God directs him to place the meal on a rock nearby and to pour the broth over the top. This was Gideon's first test of obedience. I mean, how much sense did this make? He had prepared a meal for his guests to consume. Why would he put it on a rock and then make a mess with the broth? What Gideon didn't know was that the meal was about to be consumed, but not as he expected.

After pouring the broth over the meal, Gideon stepped back. Then Jesus reached out with the staff He was holding, touched the food with the tip, and fire consumed it all. When the smoke cleared, Gideon looked up and the Lord was gone.

Gideon knew real fast he had been in the presence of the Lord. Test number one: Passed.

Truth or Dare, Level 2

Later this same day, Jesus returns and speaks to Gideon with instructions for a second test. This time, He upped the ante. This would require a higher degree of obedience.

That same night the Lord said to him, "Take the second bull from your father's herd, the one seven years old. Tear down your father's altar to Baal and cut down the Asherah pole beside it. Then build a proper kind of altar to the Lord your God on the top of this height. Using the wood of the Asherah pole that you cut down, offer the second bull as a burnt offering." (Judges 6:25, 26)

Gideon was about to make a lot of people mad. In fact, he was afraid of how his own family would respond to his "Extreme Altar Makeover." He gathered ten of his servants and carried out the Lord's instructions under the cover of night. This was Gideon's second step on the Obedience Grid. First it was extra-crispy fast food on the rock...now, he was being challenged with greater risk.

There's an old phrase that reminds me of the value of taking risks: "A turtle can only make progress after he sticks his neck out." Taking a risk is the essence of progress. For that matter, it is the essence of faith. In fact, risk and faith are dependent values – little risk requires little faith; large risk requires large faith. If we want to experience God's work in our lives, we have to be willing to push out into the deep water away from the shores of opportunity. Listen to the words of Sir Francis Drake:

"Disturb us, Lord, when we are well pleased with ourselves,
When our dreams have come true because we have dreamed too little,
When we arrive safely because we sailed too close to the shore.
Disturb us, Lord, when with the abundance of things we possess
We have lost our thirst for the waters of Life;
Having fallen in love with life
We have ceased to dream of eternity.
And in our efforts to build a new Earth
We have allowed our vision of the new Heaven to dim.
Disturb us, Lord, to dare more boldly

To venture on wider seas. where storms will show your mastery;
Where losing sight of land
We shall find the stars.
We ask you to push back the horizons of our hopes;
And to push into the future in strength, courage, hope and love."

As Gideon followed through on the command to destroy the altar and the Asherah poles, the townspeople became very angry. They just showed up and were ready to kill him. But his father, Joash, stood up and spoke on Gideon's behalf and pretty much shamed them all.

"Are you going to fight Baal's battles for him? Are you going to save him? Anyone who takes Baal's side will be dead by morning. If Baal is a god in fact, let him fight his own battles and defend his own altar." (Judges 6:31)

As the people backed down, they retreated and rallied their troops. While it wasn't clear what was about to happen next, it was clear to Gideon that God was up to something big. He had seen God burn up the food, and now God had protected him in the face of death. Gideon had passed two levels on the Obedience Grid, and now God was about to take him even further.

As the Midianites and the Amalekites assembled together across the river, Gideon knew it was time to prepare for battle. Armed with a new level of confidence, Gideon sounded the alarm for fellow warriors to come join him in preparation for battle. This is quite the turnaround for Gideon. He went from hiding in the winepress to preparing to lead tens of thousands into battle. There's something to be said for small victories. When we have success in small things, they set us up for larger ones along the way.

However, oftentimes the victory is not so much

connected to the outcome as it is to obedience in the face of uncertainty. Gideon did not know where his obedience was taking him. For him, the victory was in the obedience, not in the burned up food or in building a new altar. When you and I are obedient in the "small" things, God can begin to trust us with larger opportunities. I love John Maxwell's thought on this: "God will give to you what He knows will flow through you."

Have you had a moment when you were pretty sure God was compelling you to do something a little out of the ordinary? Maybe speak to someone you didn't know or give away something to someone who had a need? It's a moment that we really can't explain. There's something inside of us saying, "You need to _____." It is moments like this that help us determine how strong our faith and obedience really is.

Craig Groeschel brought this to light for me in his talk at the 2012 Catalyst conference. Craig enlightened the audience as he brushed us up on our Greek by introducing the phrase, "deo ho pneuma" which means "compelled by the Spirit" or "compelled by God." It's those moments where God will want to know if we're willing to obey and follow Him. How we respond will have a huge impact on our present and our future.

These moments can be as simple as Gideon's fast-food experience or as complex as his leading of thousands into battle. Regardless of the magnitude, they all turn on one component: obedience. I know from personal experience, that obedience has a determined foe: fear.

When I was a college student, I attended a conference hosted by Campus Crusade for Christ. I don't remember a lot of details about the conference. I could not tell you who the musical artist was or who any of the speakers were. What I do remember is that during a break I experienced my personal "deo ho pneuma" moment as I had a personal conversation with God. It was not an audible conversation, but a moment where it seemed there was no one in the auditorium except the two of us, even though we were surrounded by hundreds of college students.

The conversation went something like this:

God: So, what are you planning to do with your life?
Me: Oh, you know, Lord, I'm going to be a teacher.
God: Ah...So you have it all figured out?
Me: Sure! Remember, we worked this all out a few years ago. (That's another story...)
God: How about this...How about you letting me take it from here?
Me: (long silence) Uh...What do you have in mind?
God: This can't be a negotiation. I need to know that you will trust me with the results. I need to know you are ready for whatever I have in store.
Me: "Whatever?"
God: Whatever...
Me: (another long silence) But "whatever" is whatever...Right?
God: (no response)
Me: Right? (I knew the answer. I was just stalling.)

Some say silence is golden, but I wasn't feeling very golden at that moment. I sat there in silence and began to consider what I was being asked to do. He wanted me to commit "whatever" to the Creator of "whatever." If I consented, then I would be committing to whatever He had in store. That could be teaching in some remote town in the U.S. or a remote village in Africa. "Whatever" meant whatever.

Me: OK...I'm in! (Whew!) Now what?
God: I'll take care of that; you just stay the course and stay close.

At the time, I was preparing to be a math teacher. Today, I strive to help people connect with God and leverage their lives for His glory. Along the way, I've had the opportunity to travel to various parts of the world and the US teaching a different curriculum, the Bible. I've been able to watch people use their lives to help others understand a bigger plan that God has for them and His desire for a relationship with Him.

Having a "deo ho pneuma" moment is part of the process of aligning our lives with God's plan. It's not fun, but when we go through the experience, we discover a plan that is a lot different from the one we have mapped out in our mind. When we are called upon to accept His plan, there will be many logical arguments as to why we need to resist. Don't resist; just relax and say, "Whatever," and watch Him do what only He can do. Don't worry about the destination; just prepare for the journey.

CHAPTER 6: FEAR, FAITH AND A FLEECE

You can't pass up a good rope swing

When I was in college, a group of friends and I were out trekking through the woods on a hot summer day near Lake Hartwell, SC. As we made our way along the bank, someone in our group said, "What's that?" We all looked up to see a rope swing dangling from a branch reaching out over the lake.

There was no question as to what to do next. We scurried over to make our ascent up this tree – the only question was who would be first to fly through the air with Tarzan-like grace into the cool, refreshing waters of Lake Hartwell? Somehow in this race of champions, I made it to the tree first and ascended to the launch site. The last guy there had the honor of retrieving the dangling rope.

As the end of the rope was passed up the tree, I began to pick the best spot for my descent. Once the rope was in hand, I gave it a tug, and –

Wait. I took the rope, gave it a tug, and...and...and...

That's right, I stood there. I was frozen on my perch, paralyzed by fear. All I could see was clip after clip on America's Funniest Videos where some brave-hearted soul attempted what I was about to do, and it had ended very badly. At least none of my friends was sporting a video camera.

Can you imagine the battle waging inside my head? It was courage versus fear. Part of me couldn't wait to launch myself into the air while the other part saw everything that could go wrong. This is where Gideon found himself. As confident as Gideon appears at the end of his encounter with the Lord, after making it through the obedience grid, we discover real quickly that he's not so sure.

Gideon said to God, "If you will save Israel by my hand as you have promised— look, I will place a wool fleece on the threshing floor. If there is dew only on the fleece and all the ground is dry, then I will know that you will save Israel by my hand, as you said." And that is what happened. Gideon rose early the next day; he squeezed the fleece and wrung out the dew—a bowlful of water. Then Gideon said to God, "Do not be angry with me. Let me make just one more request. Allow me one more test with the fleece, but this time make the fleece dry and let the ground be covered with dew."40 That night God did so. Only the fleece was dry; all the ground was covered with dew (Judges 6:38-40)

Truth or Dare, God's Turn

Gideon quickly turned into a negotiator twice. Not only did he challenge God once, but he also twisted it up just to make sure God was listening. The good news is that God accepted Gideon's' "Truth or Dare" challenge and made it clear that He had great plans for Gideon. Yet, Gideon was about to allow fear to prevent him from experiencing what God had in store for him.

All men are driven by faith or fear – one or the other. Both are beliefs we have about an event that hasn't happened yet. Faith says, "With God's help, I've got this" while fear says, "I don't think I can do this." You can trace it all back to how big your God is. Big God, little fear; little God, big fear.

We can't run from the things that paralyze us with fear. When we run from fear, we run into regret. So our only option is to turn toward that which strikes fear in our gut and take one step in that direction… then another…and another. Just like Gideon, we'll discover small victories along the way that will eventually lead to a great victory.

Courage Is Not the Absence of Fear

The truth is we will always come face to face with fear. It's unavoidable. Our choice is to decide what we will fear most. Will we be more afraid of missing out on what God has in store or more afraid of making a mistake? We can usually recover from a mistake, but while God is full of grace, some decisions about the course of our lives tend to be permanent. You never really recover from missed opportunities. They tend to haunt you for the rest of your life.

This is why we are called to walk by faith and not by sight. Our tendency is to wait for opportunities to unfold before we act. Many want God to give them great opportunities first; then they step out on "faith." We want to know we'll win the race before we ever take the first step of training. We have more doubt than we have faith. This is where courage becomes critical. Courage is that thing inside you that compels you to act even when you don't know the results. But it sure is easier knowing that the Lord is your safety net.

JP, the Flyer

Some friends of mine, Scott and Wendy, were remodeling the exterior of their home and decided to build a new back porch. Due to the slope of their backyard, the distance from the floor of the porch to the ground was an easy fifteen feet. It turned out to be more than the "Weekend Project" they expected it to be.

As the construction began, there was an additional challenge of their three-year-old curious and adventurous son, JP. He wanted to watch the project from beginning to end. As Scott took a break to go down to ground level to gather some more supplies, he noticed JP had ventured out onto the porch. As any parent would do, he looked up and cautioned JP to stay back from the edge, since they had not yet added any railing.

Scott then returned to determining what materials he needed and thought to direct his attention back to JP's observation deck. Turning around to check his position on the porch, Scott was greeted instantly by the soaring body of his son, who had taken flight from above. Scott was fortunate to be empty-handed and quick in his reflexes. In the matter of milliseconds, he opened his stance and caught JP in his arms.

Once the shock wore off, Scott turned JP around to make the obvious point that what he did was very dangerous and could have ended much worse. In his scolding he asked, "Why would you jump from that high in the first place?" The answer could only come from a child. JP said, "I knew you would catch me, Dad."

We need this kind of faith. A faith that says to God, "I

knew you would catch me, Dad."

Where there is doubt, there is no faith

James 1:6 reads, "But when you ask, you must believe and not doubt, because the one who doubts is like a wave of the sea, blown and tossed by the wind."

Have you ever not attempted something because you doubted that you could be successful or were afraid you would fail? Some would say that the moment you listen to your fears is the moment you fail. Which means we allow fear to determine the where, when, and how of what we attempt for the Lord. Just like me standing in that tree, we allow fear to paralyze us and render us ineffective.

Far too often we filter life through what we can't do rather than what we can. This typically leads to a lack of confidence in us and, unfortunately, God as well. This is the birthplace of doubt. We are challenged to choose between leaning on the possibilities of what God can do with our lives or doubting He can do anything at all. In essence the size of our fear will announce the size of our God.

The Circle of Confidence

We all have a degree of confidence in our abilities. We know there are some things we're very capable of doing. Let's use a circle to illustrate our confidence. Inside the circle are those things we know we can do well. This is what many call their "Comfort Zone." When we consider these qualities or activities, we find no fear in how God can and will use them for His glory. There's not a lot of faith required inside the circle. Then there's that area outside the circle. I like to refer to this as the "Growth

Zone." This is where we grow our faith.

How big is your circle? Can it get any larger? It's not God's plan for our circle to stay the same size forever...right? Otherwise, why would we need faith? Why would we need Him?

God wants us to enlarge our circle. He is constantly giving us opportunities to attempt new things that require us to get out of our comfort zone and trust Him with the results. Why? It's because He wants us to gain a greater knowledge and experience of His power and faithfulness. The challenge for us is to not push back from those moments, but to embrace them as opportunities to grow, no matter how uncomfortable or awkward we might feel.

But there's still this fear of failure that you have to defeat.

It's all about perspective. You have to move away from seeing the consequences to seeing the possibilities. The mere fact that there are no perfect people should let you know that failure is common. The difference in people is that some see failure as defeat, and others see it as victory. I recently heard John Maxwell say that in life, "there are winners, and there are learners." Henry Ford said, "Failure is the opportunity to try again, this time more intelligently."[1]

Don't follow Gideon's path. If you feel like there's something God is preparing you to do for His glory, don't push back. Don't let fear of failing keep you from experiencing the blessing of seeing Him do a great work in your life. Even if you don't "succeed," you stand a good chance of growing in your faith and discovering a level of intimacy with God that you never knew before.

To Germany and back in 300 days

Randy Hahn is the pastor of Colonial Heights Baptist Church in Colonial Heights, Virginia. God is doing a great work at CHBC under Randy's leadership. But Colonial Heights almost missed the opportunity to experience what God is doing.

Randy wasn't always on course to be a pastor. There was a period of time when Randy and his wife, Karen, found themselves wrestling with a call to reach people in another part of the world. Through a series of events, God changed "the plan" and opened a door for them to devote their lives to sharing the Gospel of Jesus Christ with the people of Germany.

This didn't make sense. It was clear that God was blessing them as they prepared to eventually be a pastor and pastor's wife. God had positioned them in a large church to serve and learn all they could about leading and serving people. Their children were young and would make friends no matter where they served. They had matured into a great couple who could do great things in God's hands. How did overseas mission work ever get on the radar? The real story is what happened after they began the journey of going to Germany.

The process of preparing for this new venture was both exciting and challenging. The mission organization they chose to help guide them was very thorough in their interviews. It seemed at times that they were discouraging Randy and Karen from following the Lord to be missionaries in Germany. Eventually, it would be clear that this was just part of the process to help candidates confirm the call to serve overseas, and through this process, it became even more clear that this was the next step for Randy and Karen. They persisted in their plans for leaving, began announcing their departure, and prepared for Germany. They even sold their home.

Through all of the conversations and questions, they not only surrendered to the change of plans, but they had begun to develop an attachment to the people they would soon be serving. Despite the circumstances of how they had begun this new journey, they began to see how God had used several opportunities to prepare them for where they were headed.

Then it all changed. The Hahns were no longer destined for Germany. In fact, they weren't destined for anywhere. One moment they were preparing to clean out their home, move their family and begin learning German. The next moment, they were trying to figure out how to explain to so many people that they weren't going anywhere. It was as if God said, "Hold that thought." It was akin to Abraham's charge to sacrifice Isaac, only to be stopped at the last moment.

While they didn't know why God had taken them down this seemingly dead-end road, they experienced His faithfulness and grace like never before. There was no doubt in their minds that He was building a bigger plan for them. And while this journey had not taken them to the destination they had in mind, they were ready for what would come next. Randy's perspective about this is very simple: "What a reminder that God always knows where He is going and where we are going, but He doesn't mind throwing a curve in the road to see if we are following."

Soon after this experience, Colonial Heights Baptist Church came calling, and now the Hahns are seeing God do amazing things. In the ten years the Hahns have been at CHBC, the church has relocated, built a new campus, grown from 800 people to 2400 people, and will soon launch two satellite campuses. How this all connects to a call to go serve the people in Germany, we may never know. But the lesson here is simple: When God compels you to do something, you have more to gain in your obedience than to lose in your disobedience.

We all need a good dose of fear

Fear is not something to be totally avoided. Fear can be healthy for our faith. When we find ourselves facing an uncertain future with the potential of unfavorable consequences, it reminds us of our need for God's intervention in our lives. We remember quickly how small we really are and how much we need His help.

And yet, something happens when we come face-to-face with fear. It marks us. We come out of our circumstances different than before we were confronted with uncertainty. We have a different perspective of God. His faithfulness during our battle with fear makes us walk differently and talk more confidently.

One reason for this is that we have stared fear in the face and decided where we would place our trust. We will either trust our own abilities or God's. I think our odds of trusting God are better, but we have to keep our minds engaged in this battle, or fear will overpower us before we ever begin.

When Nick Walenda walked a tight-rope across Niagara Falls, he looked cool as a cucumber. But in an interview afterwards, he shared that fear was a constant obstacle for him. As he put it, "I have to really monitor how much [fear] I take into my own mind."[2] I think it's safe to say that no matter who you are, when you're in a circumstance where death is a possible outcome, you're going to deal with fear. But even if death is not the risk, the key is to not allow fear to dominate you, leaving you crippled, living life wondering, "What if?"

Dying to take risk

How many times have you found yourself "frozen on a perch" due to fear of the unknown? When I stood on that limb at Lake Hartwell, I was about to enjoy the laws of physics as I would launch myself into the air, defying gravity for just a few seconds, only to land in a cool, refreshing lake on a hot summer day. Instead, I was standing in a tree, rocking back and forth, listening to the "encouragement" of my peers. All because I wasn't willing to take a risk.

I once read where a research firm had conducted a survey of a large group of people who matched just one criteria: they had to be ninety-five years or older. They asked this group just one question. The question was, "If you could live your life over, what would you do differently?" The number one answer was, "I would take more risks."

Marketing guru, Seth Godin, makes the point that there is a big difference between an "Idea" and an "I did." I would contend that the difference is that the "I did" people faced their fears and took risks, while the "Idea" people ran from them. Facing our fears will help us move beyond our ideas and grow our faith.

What risk do you need to take? Where do you need to exercise your faith? Regardless, don't get caught standing in a tree thinking about all the ways you can fail.

Oh, that reminds me...I eventually mustered up my courage and launched myself out of the tree. While the trip to the lake may have been graceful, the landing was a flop – a belly flop that stung all over my body. But the coolness of the water and the satisfaction that I had defied my fears made me forget how bad it hurt. From that point on, I never hesitated on all of my other trips out of the tree.

CHAPTER 7: MY PLAN LIMITS HIS POSSIBILITIES

If you haven't figured it out by now, I'm challenging you to live a life that's more than what you are expecting...or is it to expect more from the life you're living? No matter how we say it, we must realize God did not create us to be fully satisfied by our own means. In fact, His plan is greater than anything we can dream up on our own. It is truly outrageous.

Ephesians 3:20 says it best: "Now to him who is able to do immeasurably more than all we ask or imagine, according to his power that is at work within us." God's desire is that His possibilities exceed our plans. When we rely solely on our plans, we restrict the outcomes to what can only be described by logic. We were created to see and experience more than our minds can dream up.

The problem is that most of us are like the elephant who's been tied to a peg its entire life. It started out as a metal chain that kept us from wandering off. Eventually, it turned into a rope. While we have all the strength and ability to break free, we've become accustomed to limitations and never think that we could actually move out further than we perceive.

It's a Hard Habit to Break

Even greater contributors to our stifled lives are the habits we form. Our habits can create barriers or accelerators in our lives. Barriers keep us from becoming what God planned for us. Accelerators put us on the fast-track to what God has in store.

Habits are those behaviors that we develop over time and eventually execute without any thought or hesitation. As much as they can be contributors to our personal lives, they also make us very predictable. Let's take a test:

- Choose a number between 2 and 9.
- Multiply that number by 9.
- Take the digits of this answer and add them together.
- Using your new number, subtract 5.
- Associate your new number with a corresponding number of the alphabet: 1 = A, 2 = B, etc.
- Using this letter, think of the name of a country that begins with that letter.
- Using the last letter of the name of this country, think of an animal.
- Finally, using the last letter of the name of this animal, think of a color.

Because we're creatures of habit, our decisions are predictable. If that weren't true, then why would you have a fascination with Orange Kangaroos from Denmark? (If you have some other "fascination," you must be unique.)

Two's Company – 32,000 Is a Crowd

Gideon shared our tendency to default to habits. The habit of choice was to make a plan. All throughout our experience with Gideon, we've seen his skepticism and doubt. That leads me to believe that Gideon relied first on his own ability before even considering what God could do. We see a great example of this from Scripture.

Early in the morning, Jerub-Baal (that is, Gideon) and all his men camped at the spring of Harod. The camp of Midian was north of them in the valley near the hill of Moreh. The Lord said to Gideon, "You have too many men. I cannot deliver Midian into their hands, or Israel would boast against me, 'My own strength has saved me.' Now announce to the army, 'Anyone who trembles with fear may turn back and leave Mount Gilead.'" So twenty-two thousand men left, while ten thousand remained. But the Lord said to Gideon, "There are still too many men. Take them down to the water, and I will thin them out for you there. If I say, 'This one shall go with you,' he shall go; but if I say, 'This one shall not go with you,' he shall not go." (Judges 7:1-4)

God called Gideon to gather the people who would fight the Midianites and Gideon obeyed. Gideon did what made sense. He gathered the biggest and "baddest" army possible. The problem was that he had too many for God to do something great. And that's what God wanted to do – something outrageous! I don't think God is so much concerned about our success as He is about how His name can be glorified. If we have a battle to fight where we can plan for success, then why do we need God?

So God told Gideon that He would narrow the field. I'm sure He knew that if He left it up to Gideon, he would still play it safe.

So Gideon took the men down to the water. There the Lord told him, "Separate those who lap the water with their tongues as a dog laps from those who kneel down to drink." Three hundred of them drank from cupped hands, lapping like dogs. All the rest got down on their knees to drink. The Lord said to Gideon, "With the three hundred men that lapped I will save you and give the Midianites into your hands. Let all the others go home." So Gideon sent the rest of the Israelites home but kept the three hundred, who took over the provisions and trumpets of the others. Now the camp of Midian lay below him in the valley. (Judges 7:5-8)

Now, that's a change of scenery. Gideon went from being surrounded by 32,000 fighting men and a lot of confidence to looking at 300 men and a lot of questions. How was this going to work? What would he do with all of the extra food? How could they possibly defeat the Midianites? This is exactly where God wants us: facing questions without answers; He not only wants to be responsible for the answer. He wants to be the answer.

Plan Your Work and Work Your Plan

When we are faced with challenges or obstacles in our lives, we tend to be like Gideon and formulate our own plan and strategy for success. It's in our DNA.

"In their hearts humans plan their course..." (Proverbs 16:9)

We can't help but start planning out the actions we need to take to achieve success. And yet, the bottom line is that we can't get far without the Lord's involvement.

"In their hearts humans plan their course, but the Lord establishes their steps." (Proverbs 16:9)

God knows He must be a part of our plans because, left fending for ourselves, we wouldn't get very far. If we lived life solely by our plans, our lives would be very safe and futile. In fact, if we accomplish our plans just as we position them, we only set ourselves up for pride and self-realization. And when we do that, we say to God, "I don't need your help," which may sound sufficient for the moment, but will eventually lead us to a place where we have no control. When this happens, we will become keenly aware that He is the only one who can rescue us, but our pride will hinder our prayers and pleas for help.

This is why He must be a part of what we want to accomplish in life. Our ultimate goal should be to align our plans and dreams with His and allow Him to direct us to even greater opportunities. We must come to grips with the fact that His plans are greater than ours. God wants to be a part of our plans, not because He wants to take over, but because He wants to use them to shape us into the individuals He created us to become. He also wants us to witness His power in and through us to do great works.

All through Scripture, you read story after story of how God used men and women to accomplish great things. He used Moses to deliver the Israelites from Egypt, Joshua to lead them into the land God had promised their ancestors, and Nehemiah to rebuild the city walls after the Babylonians had captured them. In the New Testament, God used a quaint couple to be the earthly parents of His son, twelve least-likely candidates to train and prepare to be messengers of His resurrection, and a Jewish ruler who was known for his persecution of Christians to raise up new churches and leaders in order to extend the Gospel to other parts of the world.

God has a way of using unlikely men and women to accomplish things they never thought or imagined. Most of the time, we think we have a good plan, but as the chapter title communicates, our plans limit God's possibilities. It's only when we step back and look up that He can begin to do something really amazing.

Waiting List

Caz McCaslin is the president and founder of Upward Sports. He knows firsthand how our plans are so much smaller than God's plans. The key is to follow His plan over our own. Caz strongly adheres to the truth in Ephesians 2:10, which reads, "For we are God's handiwork, created in Christ Jesus to do good works, which God prepared in advance for us to do." After witnessing God doing something greater than he ever imagined, Caz has a great story to share of how God's vision for his life exceeded his own.

In 1986, Caz began a church youth basketball league, which he named Upward Basketball. The church where he served as the Recreation Minister had a simple place to play basketball. While other churches had a CLC (Christian Life Center), ROC (Recreation Outreach Center) and a MAC (Ministry and Activity Center), his church just had a G-Y-M.

The model for the league seemed to meet a need in the community. They maxed out at 480 kids playing basketball. Even after making some slight adjustments to the schedule to allow for more teams, they maxed out again at 520 kids. It was very clear that God was blessing the plans Caz had committed to Him.

The following season, the buzz about Upward Basketball started early and people started calling asking to register, but they all had to wait for "Opening Day." When Upward finally opened registration, they had a flood of parents on their doorstep. This is enough to make anyone excited about what God was up to. It was also a canyon of temptation as one could look at what was going on and take credit for it all. That's what Caz did as he rushed home to tell his wife, "Baby, you won't believe what happened today. We closed the registration with 520 kids, and we have 27 kids on a waiting list." Her response? "Well, Honey, if it was your goal to put 27 kids on a waiting list, then you did good." There wasn't much conversation after that.

Not What You Expect a Preacher to Say

Two weeks later, Caz's church brought in a guest speaker to spend some time learning about how they operate and find some ways to encourage them to connect with more people in the community. The speaker was delayed and only showed up in time to speak to the group of church leaders assembled for a dinner. He began his talk with this question: "Why does your church have a Children's Ministry, a Youth Ministry, or a pastor who stands behind a pulpit and preaches the word every Sunday?" That's a fair question. After several suggestions, he got the answer he was looking for: "To reach people with the Gospel of Jesus Christ." He spent the next 45 minutes challenging them with the thought that if people were coming to their church, and there was not a place for them to sit and hear the Gospel, then the church had denied them that opportunity solely because there wasn't a place for them to sit.

Then the talk took an unexpected turn for Caz. As the speaker was making his point, he ended with this statement: "I don't know a lot about your church. I don't know if you have a youth room, a nursery, a children's ministry, a choir, or how many people you can sit in your sanctuary. But if you so much as have a gym and you're turning kids away from playing basketball, you might as well place a big yellow flashing sign in front of your gym that reads, 'Go to Hell! We're full!'"

Caz never heard a thing after that. In fact, he got up, left the room and ran to his car with his wife chasing behind. Caz sat in his car sobbing over the steering wheel as his wife asked the obvious question, "What are you going to do?" The answer came back, "Whatever it takes."

A Hidden Gem...I Mean Gym

The next day, Caz launched a quest to find more space. As he wandered around the church, he ended up in the student worship room and had an epiphany. The place where the Middle School and High School students worshiped was once the church gym. He called the Student Minister in and shared his story and a plan. If they made a few modifications and agreed to share, they could make room for more kids to play basketball. Caz had a good plan, but there was one hurdle neither of them could clear: funding. Neither had the money in their budget to cover the cost of the necessary renovations. But Caz had another plan.

Proverbs 15:22 reads, "Plans fail for lack of counsel, but with many advisers they succeed." Caz had a group of men he confided in for wisdom and guidance throughout his life. With a plan and some estimates, Caz went to see one of these men.

Caz shared how God had blessed the league even leaving 27 kids on a waiting list. He also shared how God had rocked his world with the guest speaker. Finally, he sought wisdom with the plan he had developed to get those 27 kids into the league and any more who might want to play. The gentleman listening to this story agreed that Caz had a good plan in place and asked what he could do to help. Caz's response was, "I need you to help me get this through the Building Committee, the Deacons, the Church Staff, and then the Pastor." His friend said, "Caz, this is a Baptist church." It was very obvious that to pull that off in the amount of time they had would almost be impossible. This gentleman made a very wise decision and reached into his desk, pulled out a checkbook, and wrote a check to cover the necessary expenses for Caz's plan.

In a matter of days, they had painted walls, purchased new carpet and installed new goals. They opened registration and added 200 more kids, with 27 playing for free. It was a very exciting time in the church, but not for Caz. With the addition of these 200 kids, the league was now full again. What would he do now?

We Need Another Gym

As Caz pondered his next step, he began to think about the possibility of building a second gym. Another gym would allow for another 500 kids to sign up to play. He asked an architect friend to take a casual look at what it would take to make space for another gym right next to the existing one. The results came back very positive. They would only lose 35 parking spaces, and using some of the existing gym would keep costs much lower than an entire free-standing gym. With plans under his arm and all the excitement he could contain, Caz went back to see his friend.

Caz began to share a vision of reaching 500 more kids

and their families. He rolled out the plans from the architect and showed how knocking down a wall and taking away only 35 parking spaces would give them all the space they needed and more. Then came the obvious question, "How much would something like this cost?" Caz was excited to announce, "Two point three million dollars." But Caz didn't stop there, "Would you like to borrow my pen?"

Silence fell over the room. Caz's friend sat down and pushed back from his desk and responded, "Caz, you don't need another gym." Caz felt the energy leave the room. His friend had lost the vision. He did not see how the plan was going to work. Then his friend looked him straight in the eye and said, "Caz, you need a thousand gyms. I want you to write the book on how to create the level of excellence you have in Upward Basketball and empower other churches to share the love of Jesus Christ through a basketball."

Right then, Caz saw how small his plans were. That day his vision went from building a gym to accommodate 500 more kids to a ministry that has currently seen 4.5 million kids around the globe play Upward Basketball and more.

Our plans limit God's possibilities. What plans are you making well within your reach that may be limiting what God can do both in and through you? Put them to the side and chase hard after God to see what He has in store. I feel confident that it will be much better than what you had in mind. It will be outrageous.

CHAPTER 8: HIS PLAN IS TO REFLECT AND DEFLECT

Before we see the rest of the story, I want to back up to a short verse you may have passed over in your haste to see how this story ends. It's not a long verse, but it's one of the most important ones:

The LORD said to Gideon, "You have too many men. I cannot deliver Midian into their hands, or Israel would boast against me, 'My own strength has saved me.'" (Judges 7:2)

The ultimate end-goal in all of Gideon's experiences is that God's name would be elevated before all who were involved...from the people who were angered when Gideon destroyed the altar, the thousands who responded to the battle cry only to be sent home, and the Midianites who were terrorizing the Israelites. This is the chief-end of life: Bring honor and glory to God.

1 Corinthians 10:31 makes it clear, "So whether you eat or drink or whatever you do, do it all for the glory of God." When you drill down on the Greek for the word "glory" as it's used here, you discover it means "a most exalted state." In other words, there is no one above God

for whom we should do anything. All we do should be done to direct others to His amazing love and power.

Brent Crowe puts a spotlight on this concept in his book, Chasing Elephants. He shares, "A follower of God is to live as if the purpose of his entire existence is for the present moment. As living sacrifices, we should seek to capture each moment of life to the glory of God as if that moment were the last opportunity we'd have to do so."[1] How many opportunities have you had to give God the credit for what's happened in your life?

Gideon was faced with such an opportunity, and, like so many of us, had figured out how to make it work. But God put it so well, "You have too many men." In other words, Gideon had a good plan, but that was the problem – it was Gideon's plan. If they had followed his plan and won the battle, he and Israel would have taken credit for the victory. If life were about us and our plans, then would we even need God? We need to remember the reason God made man in the first place.

Genesis 1:26 says, "Let us make man in our image." We were created to reflect the image of God to those around us. When God uses us to do something great and we attempt to take credit for it, we're only reflecting ourselves. I don't know about you, but I'm pretty sure people are not very interested in my image.

Our goal should be to reflect and deflect. When God uses our lives to accomplish something great, and those around us want to pour on the praise, our goal should be to reflect God's character in how we perform and then deflect the praise to Him – Reflect and Deflect.

Our current culture has many examples of what this looks like. The most notable are professional athletes. We see many who will gesture in some way as to indicate visually they are honoring God, but the ones who put it on the line are the ones who use their words to give credit to the Lord. To be standing in front of a group of media outlets and answer questions is intimidating in itself, but to be able to deflect the credit and praise for what has happened in your life takes boldness and commitment to spending time in God's Word.

Matthew 5:18 teaches us that the words that come out of our mouths come from the overflow of our hearts. In other words, whatever content we are putting into our lives will be revealed by the words we use in our conversations. A commitment to putting the Bible into our hearts helps prepare us for the opportunities we'll have to boast about the Lord. The prophet Jeremiah reminds us, "But let the one who boasts boast about this: that they have the understanding to know me, that I am the Lord, who exercises kindness, justice and righteousness on earth, for in these I delight," declares the Lord." (Jeremiah 9:24)

When Mom Takes the Microphone

You never know when the opportunity will unfold for you to reflect and deflect of God's behalf. My daughter was invited to a Spring Sports Award Banquet for athletes in our state of South Carolina. As part of the program, they were going to present the "Mr. Baseball" award for the best player in our state. The emcee called the names of the finalists and asked the parents and players to make their way to the stage. Based on the expressions and body language of the parents, this was a surprise. They were there to support their sons, not to be in the spotlight. The emcee began to move toward each trio as he provided some key stats for the young men standing with their parents. He commented on how challenging it was to reduce the list of finalists down to just one player. In an attempt to help the audience identify with each young man, he made a request of the parents to share something about their son as he shoved the microphone into the face of the mom standing in front of him.

Silence.

Again, it was very obvious that this was not pre-arranged and that these parents were more on the spot than in the spotlight. The first mom had it the worst. At least the others were going to have a few minutes to mentally arrange their words. It's in times like this when Matthew 5:18 really comes to light. The first mom didn't have minutes, she had seconds, but she didn't flinch.

In a slightly trembling voice, she shared, "I've told my son from the time he was in middle school that regardless of what he did with baseball, he needed to keep Jesus Christ first in his life. Baseball may come and go, but Jesus will be with you until the end." Applause filled the room. Wow! Out of the overflow of the heart, the mouth speaks. Again, Brent Crowe speaks this very clearly as he shares, "Glorifying God isn't about the size of your actions or the significance of your successes: rather it's about the surrender of your heart."[2]

You've Got Two Seconds

Have you ever had a moment in your life when you felt as if you were playing a game of Musical Chairs and when the music stops, there are no more chairs?

In the context of the game, it's a simple rush of disappointment as you realize you're "out." In the context of life, it's not so simple. When you "run out of chairs" in life, everything stops. You feel as if all the oxygen has left the room. You are aware of nothing going on around you except the one thing that has stopped the music. This is what happened to David and Laurie Whitaker.

They are a great couple who had plans like many to have a family and watch their kids grow up. With child number one growing into a precious young lady, it was time to welcome another child into their family — another precious little girl. As the pregnancy progressed, some early assessments revealed the baby growing inside Laurie's womb would have a Club Foot. There was no need for alarm. This would be a "minor" challenge at first, but it could be corrected with surgery later in life. However, a few days after she was born, the music stopped. She had an extra chromosome. She had Down Syndrome.

As her parents shared her story, her dad made this comment: "It's times like this that you have just two seconds — two seconds to decide how you will respond." He shared how he was speechless with nothing to say. His wife, however, didn't flinch. With a hint of fear and a heap of faith, she asked, "Okay, where do we go from here?"

While it may have felt as if the music had stopped, she knew it was just beginning. She knew the Creator makes no mistakes. She knew this precious little girl was just as she was created to be. She knew the Creator had a plan. She had the Word in her heart and it came out of her mouth.

"I praise you because I am fearfully and wonderfully made; your works are wonderful, I know that full well. My frame was not hidden from you when I was made in the secret place. When I was woven together in the depths of the earth, your eyes saw my unformed body. All the days ordained for me were written in your book before

one of them came to be." (Psalm 139:14-16)

The bottom line here is that there will always be events in our lives over which we have no control. At those moments, the only thing we can control is our response. Will we use these moments to give God the glory He deserves, or will we take full responsibility for the results and the credit that goes with it?

Get ready. Life is moving on but one day, the music might stop. Get ready. You've got two seconds.

I Am My Worst Enemy

As you consider where you might begin to reflect and deflect, allow me to caution you about the alternative. Just as God shared with Gideon, the danger is failing to acknowledge God's role in our lives and taking credit for all we accomplish. Let me remind you how God put it to Gideon:

"I cannot deliver Midian into their hands, or Israel would boast against me, 'My own strength has saved me.'" (Judges 7:2)

The danger in taking credit for our accomplishments is the onset of pride. It's hard to see pride in the mirror, and if left unchecked, it's clearly recognizable to those around us. Pride says, "If it weren't for me, this would have never happened." This is why God wanted to limit the number of warriors He would use to fight this battle. He knew the Israelites would take credit for the victory. He also knew that the more they leaned to their own ability, the less they would lean to Him. The less they leaned to Him, the further they would go away from Him. And the further away from Him they were, the less they could reflect His image. They would only be holding themselves up for everyone to see. That attitude doesn't get you far.

Gideon Gets It

After watching his soldiers dwindle from 32,000 to 300, Gideon was now in a position where he had to rely on God one hundred percent. At this point, he could either mentally surrender to defeat and death or give all he had and see what God would do, which was a good strategy because God wasn't finished with His battle plan.

During that night, the Lord said to Gideon, "Get up, go down against the camp, because I am going to give it into your hands. If you are afraid to attack, go down to the camp with your servant Purah and listen to what they are saying. Afterward, you will be encouraged to attack the camp." So he and Purah his servant went down to the outposts of the camp" (Judges 7:9-11).

As they approached one of the tents they overheard two men having a conversation about a dream one of them had during the night. The contents of the dream revealed to Gideon that victory was his. He only needed to stick to the Reflect and Deflect plan. He returned to his camp and gave his 300 soldiers clay pots, trumpets, torches, and these instructions:

"Watch me," he told them. "Follow my lead. When I get to the edge of the camp, do exactly as I do. When I and all who are with me blow our trumpets, then from all around the camp blow yours and shout, 'For the Lord and for Gideon'" (Judges 7:17-18).

Like a football team about to score the winning touchdown, they broke their huddle with a sense of confidence and strength, and then encircled the camp. They positioned themselves as Gideon commanded them and waited for the signal. Then, at a moment when he had that gut feeling, Gideon blew his trumpet, smashed his clay pot and shouted, "A sword for the Lord and for Gideon!"[3] at which time the 300 soldiers did the same.

These were not quite the plans our military would draw up today.

Upon the announcement of battle, the men in the camp were engulfed with confusion. Some have said it was because they didn't know who was loyal to whom. Recall that there were Midianites, Amalekites, and others in the mix. There was also the matter of a huge herd of camels to consider. I would imagine a stampede of camels could create enough confusion in and of itself[4] (Judges 6:3-5). In the end, the Midianites fled the camp with some of Gideon's army in pursuit. The chase ended as the Midianite leaders were returned to Gideon. Well, at least their heads were returned.

It's Not About You

The outrageous life is more concerned with God getting the glory rather than the individual. If your focus is solely on getting all you can and canning all you get, then your success will only go as far as you can take it. Consider living your life in such a way that God can take it way further than you. And when he does, be quick to give Him the glory He deserves.

CONCLUSION

Could've, Would've, Should've

Life is too short to just pass through. I will not accept the notion that God created me to be average. One of my greatest fears is that I'll stand before Him one day, and He'll say something like, "You did a good job, Dwayne. However, let me show you what I wanted to do." Then He'll motion to a cloud, and a video will begin to portray the life He wanted me to live. My fear is that there are things He wants to do in and through my life, and I will miss them because of fear – or even worse, quitting.

Andy Andrews shares a great story in his book, *The Traveler's Gift*, about a character who gains access to a fictional area where all of the things that almost happened are stored – things like cures for cancer or great advances in technology that would make life so much more easier. The host for this tour makes this comment:

"In the game of life, nothing is less important than the score at halftime. The tragedy of life is not that a man loses, but that he almost wins."[5]

This is one of the driving forces in my life. It's part of the reason I wrote this book. I wanted to do something outrageous.

What Is Your Outrageous Task?

What outrageous task is God challenging you to do? What would you be willing to attempt for God if you knew you wouldn't fail? These are easy questions to hear, but hard questions to answer. Gideon has modeled that for us. Let's review what we've learned from Gideon's experience:

God is with us: Before we can do anything outrageous for the Lord, we have to make sure we're connected to Him. He made it clear to Gideon that He was with him. Gideon just needed to decide whether or not he was ready to follow God's plan and see what happened.

Our contribution is critical: When it comes to doing something outrageous, we can't sit back and wait for some mystical event to occur. I tell people often: God sent the rain, but Noah had to build the boat. Do you remember the story of Peter catching so much fish that his net could not contain all of them? All Peter did was let down his net. God was the One who filled it. We have a responsibility to do what we can with what we have and leave the rest to God.

Our obstacles will be His opportunities: Whenever we take that step of faith with God by our side, we have to expect challenges and setbacks. They will only mean defeat when we allow them to stop us where we are. When we bump up against an obstacle, we should step back and see it as God's opportunity to show off.

There will be small battles and great victories: Doing the outrageous is not a spectator sport. We have to get dirty and be willing to leave some skin on the floor. We have to be prepared to be knocked down and put in uncomfortable situations. It's just part of the growth process and will make us stronger all-around.

We will be afraid: Living the outrageous life means doing things that will raise our level of fear. And that's okay. We need a healthy level of fear to keep us dependent more on God and less dependent on ourselves. And typically, the areas where we fear the most provide the greatest opportunity for growing and strengthening our faith.

Our plans can get in the way: Too often, when we're afraid, we resort to our personal strengths. As I mentioned earlier, we plan out work and work our plan. The problem is that we tend to not plan for the outrageous. Our plans may lighten the stress of fear, but it only gets in the way of what God wants to do. Gideon started with 32,000, but God only needed 300.

The bottom line is to glorify God, not ourselves: God made each of us in His image. His desire is that all we do would point others to Him. When He allows us to be a part of what He's doing and experience something truly outrageous, we need to deflect the credit to Him.

My Outrageous Journey to This Very Moment

This project has been an interesting journey in itself. I've always wanted to write a book and others have suggested that I follow that dream, but I just didn't want to write a book as an item on a Bucket List. I have pushed back for quite some time.

That all changed this summer while I was away

speaking at a camp. One afternoon, I was preparing my slides when God stopped me and expressed to me, "It's time." Time for what?

Over the next fifteen minutes, I took a journey through Judges chapters six and seven, much like you just did. I discovered the opportunities Gideon had to be a part of something God was doing and the corresponding parallels that I've shared here. There was no laboring over phrases or moments of staring at a blank sheet of paper. It was all too easy.

Then the writing began. I did most of my writing between five and six in the morning. This was the best time to avoid interruptions, but as soon as six arrived, the solitude came to an end.

One interesting event really became a catalyst for the finished product. On the morning of November 21, 2012, I was SOAPing through Exodus 24, and nothing was catching my attention. As is my custom, I went back and read the whole chapter again, still empty. Believing God's word does not return void, I went back for a third reading and that's when I found it. The verse I was to dig down on was verse 18.

I just kept hovering there. What was the attraction to forty days? The more I dwelled on that concept, the more I felt as though I were to make a commitment for a forty-day period. But what was my commitment? Then it settled on me and became crystal clear. I was to give the next forty days to this project. I committed to work on this book for the next forty days and nights. Some days I wrote and some days I didn't. The days spent away from my laptop were given to research, interviews, and organization.

Another component of this forty-day emphasis was

that I asked a group of four friends to pray for me during this time. I even created a private group on Facebook for the five of us to share. Each night, I would post a summary of that day's activity. I am convinced their prayers made a huge impact on this project coming to fruition. Thanks, Angela, Tonya, Andrew and Daniel! And thanks go to my friend, Kathryn. She was the third person to see every word and help me refine my craft. And then Miranda took the final draft to its conclusion.

As I have worked to finish this book, my motive was very simple. I had to simply write this so that I could say that I did what God placed on my heart to do. Much like Gideon, I knew God was with me, my contribution was critical, my obstacles were His opportunities, faith was required, small battles lead to big victories, and my own plans would limit His possibilities. Still, I allowed Him to direct my steps and onward I pressed. To God be the glory for anything this book does in your life. It was His idea!

What's Next? How about you? Do you have a story of how God used your life to do the OUTRAGEOUS? I would love to hear it. In telling people about this book, I discovered many stories that should have been shared on these pages.

Send me an email (outrageous@morrismatters.com) and share your story. Who knows? There may be a follow-up to this book and your story might be one that encourages others to do the OUTRAGEOUS.

About the Author

Dwayne Morris is a blessed man of an amazing family! He and his wife, Angela are graduates from Clemson University and were married in 1991. They and their three outstanding children (Taylor, Logan, and Avery), reside in South Carolina.

In addition to being a husband and father, he is a minister, blogger, and speaker. His greatest joy comes from helping people leverage their life for the glory of God.

He has leveraged his life in many areas such as Broyhill Leadership Camps, Preteen America Program, Corporate Leadership Meetings, Extreme Kids Camps and the readers of www.MorrisMatters.com and www.michaelhyatt.com.

To connect with Dwayne, find him at any of the following:

- Email: Dwayne@morrismatters.com
- Blog: MorrisMatters.com
- Facebook: facebook.com/DwayneMorris
- Twitter: twitter.com/DwayneMorris

ACKNOWLEDGEMENTS

I am grateful for the transparency of the people who shared their OUTRAGEOUS stories with me. Here is how you can find more information about some of them and what they do:

Wallace Nix, Chosen Children Ministries
www.chosenchildrenministries.org

Caz McCaslin, Upward
www.Upward.org

Jon Estes, Woodlands Camp
www.woodlandscamp.org

Randy Hahn, Colonial Heights Baptist Church
www.chbaptist.com

Thanks to my church family of First Baptist North Spartanburg for being a part of my OUTRAGEOUS journey.
www.FirstNorth.org

End Notes

Introduction

[1] Matthew 7:21

[2] Peterson, Eugene H. The Message: The Bible in Contemporary Language. Colorado Springs: NavPress, 2002, 21 Oct. 2008 <http://www.biblegateway.com/>.

[3] Matthew 7:22

[4] Matthew 7:23

[5] Peterson, Eugene H. The Message: The Bible in Contemporary Language. Colorado Springs: NavPress, 2002, 21 Oct. 2008 <http://www.biblegateway.com/>.

[6] Crowe, Brent. Chasing Elephants: Wrestling with the Gray Areas of Life. Colorado Springs, CO: NavPress, 2010. Print.

[7] Psalm 37:4

[8] "I Am Second." I Am Second RSS. N.p., n.d. Web. 29 Dec. 2012.

Chapter 1: Backstory

[1] Genesis 1:1

[2] Genesis 1:28

[3] Genesis 15:6

[4] Proverbs 16:18, 19

Chapter 2: The Lord Is With You

[1] Judges 6:13

[2] Ephesians 2:10

[3] 2 Corinthians 12:9

[4] Jeremiah, David. The Book of Judges. Vol. 1. N.p.: Turning Point for God, 2008. Study Guide

[5] Campbell, Reggie, and Richard Chancy. Mentor like Jesus. Nashville, Tenn: B & H, 2009. Print

[6] "The Barna Group – Millions of Unchurched Adults Are Christians Hurt by Churches But Can Be Healed of the Pain. N.p., n.d. Web. 18 Dec. 2012

[7] "The Great Divorce Quotes." By C.S. Lewis. Good Reads Inc, n.d. Web. 25 Jan. 2013.

[8] 2 Samuel 7:3

[9] Luke 1:28

Chapter 3: My Contribution Is Critical

Chapter 4: My Obstacles Are His Opportunities

[1] Nichols, Peter M. "COVER STORY; 'I Am Not in a Good Place,' Michelangelo Wrote. 'And I Am No Painter,'" *The New York Times*. The New York Times, 21 June 1998. Web. 31 Dec. 2012

[2] *The Free Dictionary*. Farlex, n.d. Web. 31 Dec 2012.

[3] "Manure Jokes." Funny Jokes. N.p., n.d. Web 31 Dec. 2012

[4] *The Adjustment Bureau*. Universal, 2011

[5] Genesis 3:12

[6] Exodus 14:4

[7] Judges 6:16

[8] Drought Declared over in Southeast – USATODAY.com. *Drought Declared over in Southeast – USATODAY.com* N.p., n.d. Web 01 Jan. 2013.

[9] Goins, Jeff. *Wrecked: When a Broken World Slams into Your Comfortable Life*. Chicago: Moody, 2012. Print.

Chapter 5: Small Battles, Big Victories

Chapter 6: Fear, Faith and a Fleece

[1] *BrainyQuote*. Xplore, n.d. Web. 03 Feb. 2013.

[2] "No Fear: A High-Wire Health Habit." – Blogcritics Culture. N.p., n.d. Web. 01 Jan. 2013

Chapter 7: My Plan Limits His Possibilities

Chapter 8: His Plan Is to Reflect and Deflect

[1] Crowe, Brent. Chasing Elephants: Wrestling with the Gray Areas of Life. Colorado Springs, CO: NavPress, 2010. Print.

[2] Crowe, Brent. Chasing Elephants: Wrestling with the Gray Areas of Life. Colorado Springs, CO: NavPress, 2010. Print.

[3] Judges 7:20

[4] Judges 6:3-5

Conclusion

[5] Andrews, Andy. The Traveler's Gift. Waterville, Me.: Thorndike, 2004. Print.